trotman

getting into

Law

Edited by Carl Lygo

Getting into Law
Seventh edition

This seventh edition published in 2008 by Trotman Publishing, a division of Crimson Publishing Ltd.,
Westminster House, Kew Road, Richmond, Surrey TW9 2ND

© Trotman Publishing 2008

Editorial and Publishing Team
Editor Carl Lygo
Advertising Sarah Talbot, Advertising Sales Director

British Library Cataloguing in Publication Data
A catalogue record for this book is available from the British Library

ISBN 978 1 84455 149 1

Typeset by NewGen Imaging

Printed and bound by Bell and Bain Ltd, Glasgow

Contents

**For the latest news on Law courses, go to
www.mpw.co.uk/getintomed**

Preface

Over the past few years the number of applicants for law courses has increased enormously. Furthermore, competition for places on what might be regarded as the 'best' university courses has become more intense as students are becoming increasingly aware that employers are looking carefully at which universities their prospective employees have attended.

During the course of MPW's work advising students on their choice of university course, we have gathered together a huge amount of information on law courses and the legal profession. With the encouragement of Trotman Publishing that information has been brought together in this guide.

This edition has been substantially updated and revised by a number of people from the BPP Law Schools in London, Manchester and Leeds, and we are very grateful for their help. We would also like to thank the Law Society, the Bar Council, and UCAS. We hope that this guide will be of use to anyone considering law as a career.

MPW

January 2008

For up-to-date information on law courses, go to www.mpw. co.uk/getintolaw

About the authors

This edition of *Getting into Law* has been revised and updated by the following:

Professor Carl Lygo
Principal, BPP Law Schools in Leeds, London and Manchester
Carl read law at university and has a research Master's degree in law. He qualified as a barrister and practised in Leeds and London. Carl has taught at Leeds University, City University London and the University of East Anglia.

Jonathan Haines
Managing Director of BPP's Law School in Leeds
A city-trained solicitor with international firm Allen & Overy, Jonathan has an LLM from London University and is currently a member of the Legal Practice Course board, which oversees the Legal Practice Course.

Jill Livingstone
Lecturer in Business Law and Practice at BPP's Law School in Manchester
Jill qualified as a solicitor in 1997 and spent seven years in the corporate department of Eversheds LLP before joining BPP in April 2005.

Mandy Gill
Managing Director of BPP's Law School in Manchester
Mandy qualified as a solicitor in 1993 and has heen involved in vocational legal education since 1994.

Professor Peter Crisp
Dean of BPP Law School, London
After completing the Graduate Diploma in Law and the Bar Vocational Course, Peter practised in general Chancery work in Lincoln's Inn, specialising in property work of all kinds.

Rahim Shamji (LLB Law)

Rahim is a lecturer in Criminal Litigation, Evidence and Advocacy. He is a practising member of the bar at Mitre House Chambers, London, and a Qualified Mediator from the International Mediation Training Programme. His Areas of Practice are Crime and Human Rights.

Abigail Flack (LLB (Hons) University of London, Queen Mary College)

Abigail is a qualified lawyer. She specialised in corporate transactions and is now a lecturer in Business Law and Practice and Equity Finance at BPP Law School, London.

Nicola Zoumidou studied law at the Universities of Bristol and Fribourg (in Switzerland). After graduation, Nicola worked at an international law firm in Paris before completing her LPC in London and then trained and qualified as a solicitor at a small commercial firm in the City of London. Nicola then moved to a national firm of solicitors in the UK before deciding to join BPP. Nicola completed the STEP qualification whilst in practice and served on the Law Society's Probate Section Executive Committee from 2004 to 2007. Nicola now teaches on the Legal Practice Course at Manchester Law School.

Neil Stewart is manager of BPP College's Waterloo library. He holds Masters degrees from the University of Manchester in International Relations, and from University College, London in Library & Information Studies. He is a member of the British & Irish Association of Law Librarians.

Additional material was supplied by James Burnett, Director of Studies at Mander Portman Woodward in London. We would also like to thank contributors to the earlier editions of the book, in particular Fiona Hindle, Dr James Holland, Julian Webb, Paul Whiteside, Mike Semple Piggot, Frances Burton, Joanne Hubert and Justina Burnett,

Introduction

U nless this book has just slipped off the shelf into your hands and fallen open at this very page, you're probably reading it hoping to pick up some pearls of wisdom on whether or not you should study law. Well, read on ... This guide is intended to answer those questions you've always wanted to ask and possibly a few more that have never crossed your mind.

Broadly, there are three sections in this book:

1| A brief description of what solicitors and barristers actually do and how they fit into the scheme of the legal system (Chapter 2).
2| Ways in which you can become a solicitor or a barrister, including how to get work experience, and some flow charts to summarise that information (Chapters 3 and 4).
3| A guide to the vast range of law courses on offer, some tips on maximising your chances of winning a place on one of them, and an overview of the English Legal System (Chapters 5–8).

Don't be fooled, however, into thinking that *Getting into Law* will do all the work for you so you can put your feet up and watch *Ally McBeal* on TV!

You will still have to ...

■ Revise thoroughly and pass your exams. You can get on to a few university courses with fairly low grades, but those courses might not suit your needs. You'd be better off with higher grades and a wider choice of degree options available to you.

You should also ...

■ Do your own research. Talk to your teachers, friends, family, legal practitioners ... anyone who might know something about the legal profession. Consider carefully what type of course is appropriate for you. Or, come to that, whether you should even think about studying law in the first place.

01 An introduction to the legal profession

Most people's first impressions of the legal profession come from the glamorous world of film or television. The lawyers, usually bewigged barristers (*Kavanagh QC, Rumpole of the Bailey*), judges (*Judge John Deed*), pinstriped solicitors (*This Life*) or sometimes American attorneys (in which case truly glamorous people), stride heroically across the courtroom of life standing up for truth and justice. But what are lawyers and what do they actually do?

The term 'lawyer' is a loose one that covers barristers, solicitors, judges, in-house legal advisors, paralegals, legal executives, some civil servants and academic lawyers. In the UK, the crucial distinction to make is between the two main branches of the profession – solicitors and barristers. The essential difference between them relates to their respective rights to advocate on behalf of a client in court: traditionally only barristers were permitted to undertake advocacy on behalf of a client in the highest courts. This distinction means that law is sometimes referred to as a 'split' profession – but in fact the split is increasingly becoming blurred due to modern reforms that permit solicitors to undertake further training and then represent clients in the higher courts; more information on this is given in the paragraphs below. (The term 'attorney' is an Americanism and has no real meaning in the UK.)

■ Solicitors

Solicitors are often described as being like medical general practitioners (GPs). They deal directly with their clients and often have an ongoing professional and/or business relationship with them. Solicitors in private practice group together in law firm partnerships, with the senior solicitors being partners and the more junior solicitors being employed associates. Solicitors may deal with different aspects of the law, although increasingly they deal with specific areas of law, for example employment or family law or, in the City, with specialist areas such as syndicated loans, bonds or take overs and mergers. Generally speaking, law firms cover a wide area of legal practice; this means that in smaller firms lawyers may be required to cover a broad range of areas, whereas the larger law firms will have specialists in very narrow areas of law.

Historically, solicitors could only appear in lower courts, such as the magistrates' and county courts. These days, however, solicitors who obtain higher rights of audience can now appear in the Supreme Court and may even apply to become a QC (Queen's Counsel), although this is still rare.

■ Barristers

Barristers have traditionally been described as more like medical consultants. They are 'self employed referral professionals' who are often, although not exclusively, trial lawyers – meaning that they appear robed and wigged in court on behalf of their clients. Clients are usually referred to them by a professional advisor, often a solicitor – although reforms introduced in 2004 allow barristers to see the public directly where the Bar Council has agreed that no referral is necessary (for example in relation to tax advice when referred by an accountant).

It is usual for barristers (often called **counsel**) to specialise in certain areas of law, for example common law, criminal law, company law or tax law and so on. Barristers in private practice group together in **chambers,** sharing overheads and office support, but remaining self-employed professionals.

■ Size and make-up of the legal profession (England & Wales*)

The solicitors' profession in England and Wales is the largest branch of the legal profession. In 2006, its governing body, the Law Society (www.lawsociety.org.uk) reported that there were 131,347 registered solicitors and 104,543 of these held a practising certificate. To qualify as a solicitor you would normally be expected to complete a training contract period of employment that lasts two years. In the year to July 2006 the Law Society reported that 5751 new training contracts were registered.

More than 50% of solicitors are aged under 40, which illustrates how rapidly the profession has grown in the last 15–20 years. The solicitors' profession is divided between solicitors who work in private practice for law firms and those who work 'in-house' (ie for companies, government legal departments and so on). In 2006 there were 8926 private law firms employ 80,575 solicitors, with just over 42% of these firms based in the south-east of England employing 53% of all solicitors. Solicitors employed outside private practice amounted to 23,695.

---

* The legal profession in Scotland and in Northern Ireland differs from that in England and Wales. This book will focus on England and Wales but a few notes on Scotland and Northern Ireland are provided in Chapter 3, pages 26–7, Chapter 3, pages 32–3 and Chapter 5, page 45–6. For more information see www.lawscot.org.uk and www.lawsoc-ni.org.

The barristers' profession, known as the **Bar**, is much smaller than the solicitors' profession. According to the Bar Council (www.barcouncil. org.uk), in December 2006 there were a total of 14,890 barristers at the practising Bar. This is made up of 12,034 self-employed barristers of whom 30% were women and 10% described themselves as from ethnic minorities. A further 2856 barristers are in employed practice of whom 46% are female and 10% described themselves as from ethnic minorities. In 2006, whilst 1640 were 'called to the Bar' (see Chapter 3 for more information on this), only 552 obtained **pupillage** (the mandatory 12-month training stage for those who want to practise as a barrister).

■ Do I need a law degree?

The legal profession in England and Wales is virtually unique in **not** requiring all entrants to have a law degree. In fact, in September 2006 3467 non-law graduates embarked upon the full-time Graduate Diploma in Law programme (an intensive one-year conversion course for non-law graduates covering the essential foundations taught on a three-year law degree). Law firms and barristers' chambers typically claim to recruit around 40% of their intake from non-law graduates.

According to the Higher Education Statistics Agency (www.hesa.ac.uk), about 14,655 students obtained undergraduate law degrees in 2006. This number continues to rise each year: 13,735 students had obtained undergraduate law degrees in 2005 and 12,635 students had obtained undergraduate law degrees in 2004. However, the limited number of places available on postgraduate law courses means that many undergraduate law students do not carry on to qualify as solicitors or barristers. At the start of the 2006–07 academic year, 7705 students from all backgrounds began vocational training as a solicitor (the Legal Practice Course) and 1932 students began vocational training as a barrister (the Bar Vocational Course).

The other thing to be aware of is that not every law degree is recognised by the professional bodies as a **qualifying law degree (QLD)** – it all depends on the subjects that are studied on the course. This means that you must be careful when choosing your course: only a QLD will give exemption from the academic stage of training. The Law Society and the Bar Council keep records of which degrees are QLDs; this information is available on their websites, and there is also a list in Chapter 3.

■ Women in the legal profession

It is difficult to imagine that less than 100 years ago the legal profession was the preserve of the male. Things have changed and are still changing. Law Schools report that as many as two-thirds of all new students undertaking vocational legal training are female. About 42.5% of practising solicitors are female, and about 5.5% of solicitors are female partners. There is a feeling within the solicitors' profession that not enough female solicitors make it to partnership in some of the very large law firms.

About 33% of practising barristers are female, with 52% of new entrants undertaking pupillage being female. Whereas in the past it was difficult for females to break down the traditional barriers, today the profession is increasingly open to all.

There is still plenty of progress to be made by women in terms of judicial appointments. Only one woman has made it to the most senior Law Lord appointment, whilst roughly 10% of High Court and Circuit Judges are female. At the lower level, 25.6% of District Judges and Deputy District Judges are female. The barriers are beginning to break down in this area.

■ Entrance requirements

Law firms and barristers' chambers increasingly expect a minimum 2:1 degree and there is evidence that employers favour 'old' universities because of the use of A level grades. One postgraduate student reported recently that she found it frustrating that her A level grades were being used to dismiss her application and she was seriously considering taking her A levels again! Employers tend to favour those who have displayed a commitment to a career in law (demonstrated by work placements during holiday periods or relevant community work). Recently the former Department for Constitutional Affairs recommended that Law Schools should point out to law students how tough it is to eventually make it to become a barrister or a solicitor.

■ Student debts

A famous legal saying states that 'the law, like the Ritz, is open to all' – but the cost of qualifying as a barrister or solicitor is something that no doubt deters would-be entrants. Research at BPP Law School has revealed that the typical entrant to the profession has loans in the region of £15,000–£20,000 and that this is likely to increase as the impact of top-up fees for undergraduate courses bites. Entrants to the profession normally have to undertake at least one more year of vocational legal training before undertaking employer training (via a training contract or a pupillage). Nevertheless, according to a February 2007 study by Universities UK on the economic benefits of a degree, law graduates see a higher rate of return on their educational investment than any other students.

However, sponsorship for further study is available from law firms, barristers' chambers and the professional bodies. (The solicitors' branch of the legal profession probably offers more by way of funded training than the Bar.) Because law firms recruit 2–3 years ahead of when the training contract is due to start, you are advised to apply early! Nevertheless, students are increasingly opting to study part-time so they can partly fund themselves through the vocational training stage.

■ What if I don't want to go into the law after my degree?

Some students study law with no intention of becoming a professional lawyer. The legal knowledge and additional skills gained from a law degree are highly prized and can be applied to a number of jobs. We will look at those skills in more detail in Chapter 3. But what else can a law graduate do other than law? If you use Clive Anderson, Bill Clinton or Tony Blair as your role models the world is your oyster, but here are a few suggestions as to what the rest do ...

■ **Accountancy**
  Many aspects of accountancy relate to those found in legal practice, such as analysing large amounts of technical material, analysing and writing reports and advising clients. Law graduates are often particularly attracted by tax consultancy. Starting salaries are usually high.

■ **Administration**
  You need a methodical and precise approach as well as good written and communication skills for this job. Some administrative work is in private industry but most jobs are found in the civil service, local government, the health service, voluntary organisations and further and higher education institutions.

■ **Civil service**
  Interested in policy making and implementation? Then you might think about civil service departments with legal responsibilities such as the Home Office, HM Revenue and Customs, Ministry of Justice and Foreign and Commonwealth Office. Local authorities also value law graduates highly.

■ **Business management**
  The skills you develop from a law degree will be invaluable in the world of commerce and industry.

■ **The City and finance**
  A number of law graduates are lured into the highly paid world of investment banking and insurance where their legal background will give them an edge. But beware: competition is extremely tough for these high rewards.

In addition to the above areas, law graduates also go into legal publishing, the media, journalism (legal or otherwise), the police service, teaching, personnel and a lot more. Look at *What can I do with ... a law degree?*, published by Trotman, for more advice.

Some law graduates choose not to pursue the training to become either a solicitor or a barrister but would still like to do something legally related. They will often move into fields such as paralegal and clerking work.

Paralegals research cases, scan and collate documents.

Clerks undertake duties such as taking witness statements on behalf of solicitors' clients and conducting legal research for solicitors, barristers and others plus any administrative work that is required.

02 What do lawyers do?

Solicitors

As discussed in the previous chapter, about 77% of all practising solicitors (80,575) work in private practice for law firms; the rest work either in-house for companies or for government agencies etc. Solicitors' work is as diverse as life itself – they will be behind the scenes offering guidance to their clients on everything from train disasters to corporate takeovers. The working life varies enormously from firm to firm, for example, in a large firm it is not unusual to be engaged on one large case for several months, whereas in a small firm you may have 15 or more cases on the go at one time. This section offers some examples of the work that solicitors undertake and an overview of the types of organisation that employ them.

■ Large corporate firms

The largest law firms by turnover tend to be law firms specialising in corporate law and are usually based in London. There is a 'Magic Circle' of elite national and international law firms with bases in London that rank as some of the largest law firms in the world. This analysis is done yearly and changes slightly based on the performance of the firms from year to year. The latest commentary at the time of writing comes from *The Lawyer* which states that the Magic Circle firms are:

Clifford Chance LLP	(3892 lawyers)
Freshfields Bruckhaus Deringer	(2802 lawyers)
Linklaters LLP	(2740 lawyers)

All figures for lawyers at law firms in this chapter relate to the number of world-wide fee earners and the figures are taken from the Legal 500 at the date of writing.

Recently the legal profession has seen the emergence of a number of firms which are not quite classed as Magic Circle, but are ranked above the 'Silver Circle' of law firms, which are the new elite firms challenging the Magic Circle law firms on profit and revenue per partner calculations. The quality of clients and lawyers, overall levels of revenue, and international scope in both work and presence are also taken into account. Those firms almost within the Magic Circle and ranked above the Silver Circle are:

Allen & Overy	(2489 lawyers)
Herbert Smith LLP	(1196 lawyers)

| Slaughter & May | (759 lawyers) |
| Ashurst | (775 lawyers) |

The Silver Circle firms are:

SJ Berwin LLP	(619 lawyers)
Macfarlanes	(274 lawyers)
Travers Smith	(254 lawyers)

A recent trend has also developed for large US law firms to open branches in London, which contrasts with a less recent trend that has seen major London law firms expanding internationally. The London branches of these US law firms are developing fast, and include:

Skadden, Arps, Slate, Meagher & Flom LLP	(1923 lawyers)
White & Case	(1894 lawyers)
Latham & Watkins	(1595 lawyers)
Weil Gotshal & Manges	(1200 lawyers)
Shearman & Sterling	(963 lawyers)

In addition to the Magic Circle and Silver Circle some other major international law firms are:

DLA Piper	(4338 lawyers)
Lovells LLP	(1750 lawyers)
Norton Rose LLP	(1141 lawyers)
CMS Cameron McKenna LLP	(966 lawyers)
Simmons & Simmons	(965 lawyers)
Denton Wilde Sapte LLP	(746 lawyers)
Clyde & Co.	(556 lawyers)

Large law firms tend to offer a comprehensive service to corporate clients, covering areas like:

- Capital Markets
- Mergers and acquisitions
- Company law
- Banking/Finance law
- Financial regulatory law
- Competition law
- Employment and pensions law
- Commercial litigation
- Commercial property law
- Techonology, media and telecommunications law
- Law relating to overseas jurisdictions.

Work is often undertaken by teams, with little or no direct contact with the client. A typical area of work for a trainee involves conducting practical legal research or undertaking document work known as 'due diligence'. Starting salaries for graduates can be as high as £30,000 with the possibility of earning £55,000 on qualification.

Large corporate law firms tend to demand extremely high standards from their lawyers, who are well-known for working long hours. In exchange, however, these firms offer excellent training and it is not unusual for them to cater for your every need (gym in the basement, hairdresser, dry cleaner, shoe-shining service, beds in case you need to work through the night and need a quick snooze, somebody to get a present for your partner ... all to avoid you having to leave your desk!)

Case Study

Amrik Tumber qualified as a solicitor in 2005, aged 26 at Sykes Anderson LLP, and now works for Herbert Smith LLP, in London.

'Before graduating with LLB honours in law at Staffordshire University, I was acutely aware of my desire to work for a London-based practice on corporate transactions. I acted on this awareness by applying for training contracts in the penultimate year of my degree. Ideally, I would have undertaken work experience in a City practice and obtained that coveted training contract soon thereafter, but that was not to be!

Instead, having graduated, I undertook my LPC at the College of Law and, after numerous applications and interviews, landed a training contract with Sykes Anderson (at the time, one of the smallest legal outfits in the City). Undoubtedly, I learned a great degree at Sykes Anderson, particularly regarding client, time and transaction management and not to mention early and challenging responsibility.

What Sykes Anderson could not meet however, largely due to its size, was my desire to work on large, complex and international corporate transactions. With this in mind, on qualification I made applications to the large players in the City and eventually landed a place as a corporate associate with Herbert Smith. The rest, as they say, is history!

Although there is no escaping the high professional standards and commitment that firms like Herbert Smith demand, I have a great set of work colleagues, the environment is congenial and importantly I feel good about my career and the work I do (well, mostly!).'

Major national law firms

If London is not for you, then there are some very large national law firms with a major presence in large cities such as Birmingham, Bristol, Leeds, Manchester and Newcastle. Some of these firms also have offices abroad, or have associate offices abroad. These major national law firms include:

Eversheds	(1743 lawyers)
Pinsent Masons	(748 lawyers)

Hammonds	(591 lawyers)
Addleshaw Goddard	(578 lawyers)
Beachcroft Wansbroughs	(495 lawyers)
Irwin Mitchell	(210 lawyers)

Most of the larger law firms will sponsor students by paying their course fees for all postgraduate legal professional study and in many cases also offering a maintenance grant. Starting salaries for trainees tend to be high, with typical training contract salaries ranging from about £28,000–£35,000 per annum and some firms offering at least £50,000 upon qualification. Usually the larger law firms recruit 2–3 years ahead of when they expect the trainee to start work, and most will have a vacation placement scheme which typically takes place twice yearly, during the Easter and summer periods. As you can imagine, the large law firms tend to be massively over subscribed.

It is not unusual for a lawyer to leave a large law firm once qualified and move to a smaller firm for what is regarded as a better quality of life (ie shorter working hours).

Case Study

Jules Smith took a BA in Communication Studies and Management at the University of Leeds and gained a 2:1 Honours degree. She is now a second year trainee at Beachcroft LLP.

'After leaving university I actually began to carve out a career in journalism, but soon I realised that simply deconstructing press releases and rewriting them wasn't for me! I wanted to be able to use my brain in my work. I was first inspired to go into law when I realised how integrated with the functions of business the law really is. I am also very competitive!

I was delighted when I secured a training contact with Beachcroft LLP's Leeds office. They are one of the largest law firms nationally with prestigious offices in the big regional cities. They are a commercial practice and I joined them in September 2006. I have already completed seats in Professional Indemnity, Construction and I am currently working in Commercial Property. When I qualify, I am hoping to focus mainly on litigation as thankfully I work best under pressure, as litigation is all about pressure.

I wanted to stay in the north after graduation and I studied in Leeds with BPP Law School so was pleased to be offered a training contract in the Leeds area. I was lucky to secure my training contract fairly early on and the firm helped me with my course fees. I immensely enjoyed my studies, and am sure I made the right choice!'

■ Smaller law firms

These make up the largest number of law firms, and range in size from one solicitor ('sole practitioner') to firms with over 50 lawyers. They tend to specialise in areas more relevant to individuals than companies, or have smaller company clients. For example, on most high streets or in smaller town centres you will find at least one small firm dealing with:

- Criminal law
- Civil litigation
- Conveyancing (sale and purchase of property)
- Family law
- Employment law
- Wills and trusts.

Due to the location of their offices, they tend to be categorised as high street firms – but remember that small firms can still offer high quality corporate work if they have the clients, and every high street is surrounded by small businesses! Do not forget, that most large cities will have many small commercial firms dealing with good commercial work, which are not high street firms.

Typically a trainee solicitor in a small firm will have much more client contact from an early stage. You may still be working as part of a team, but normally you will work closely with the supervisor and, upon qualification, you will work autonomously. It is not unusual to have a high degree of responsibility, and even partnership, cast upon you early on.

The financial rewards might not be as high as those in the larger law firms – but smaller law firms tend to offer a different quality of life (ie shorter hours) and work that is more related to everyday life. Typical trainee starting salaries are around £17,000 in London and £15,000 outside London. Usually small firms do not offer any support with course fees or maintenance. Once qualified, starting salaries tend to be in the range of £18,000–£26,000 depending on the firm and area of qualification. Smaller firms tend to recruit 6–12 months ahead of when they expect the trainee to commence work with the firm.

Case Study

Gavin Henshaw, aged 29, qualified as a solicitor in 2003. He now practices at The Head Partnership just outside Reading and specialises in Family Law.

'I graduated from Sunderland University with a degree in English Studies. Midway through my final year at university I decided I should focus on what I wanted to do in the future and the law appealed

---

to me. On completing my degree, I took the Post Graduate Diploma in Law and then the Legal Practice Course.

Immediately thereafter, I trained with, and qualified at, a small firm in Chesham. Six months after qualifying I moved to my present firm and, almost four years on, I can say that this was certainly the right decision for me.

Whilst I initially thought about working in London, this was never something I seriously wanted. I was more interested in working for a smaller firm where everyone in the office knows everyone else as opposed to merely being a faceless employee. Also, in working for a smaller firm you are actively involved in dealing with cases and clients from a very early stage and, in any event, given the area in which the firm is based, I have found that the standard of the work I deal with is comparable to anything you would encounter in London.

For me, my current situation provides me with a great work–life balance and I have no intention of changing this arrangement, as it is far more important to me than any financial advantage that working in London could offer.'

■ Office-based or in the courtroom?

Traditionally the work of a solicitor has been predominantly office-based, with some undertaking advocacy work in the lower courts (mainly criminal work in the Magistrates' Court). This is still mainly the case as, in practice, solicitors can earn more money working in the office than they can waiting around at court for cases to be heard. In addition, the typical hourly charge-out rates for solicitors far exceed the average charge-out rates of barristers (for example, it is not uncommon for a junior barrister to earn £150 per day for an appearance, whereas a trainee solicitor may be charged out at over £100 per hour!) – so it is often more economical for the client to instruct a barrister to undertake court work.

Recently solicitors have been able to obtain the same right to be heard in the higher courts as barristers, known as the **Higher Rights of Audience**. Once a solicitor has obtained experience of advocacy in the lower courts, they can undertake an additional training course and, upon successful completion of it, take up the higher rights of audience. A number of solicitors have taken this path but it is still relatively unusual.

Barristers

One of the complaints about the English legal system is that lawyers are like buses: as soon as one appears, another two or three turn up as well. This impression comes from the fact that solicitors may often employ barristers to give specialist advice or to represent the client in court – so, instead of hiring only one lawyer, the client now has at least two on their hands. This section will outline what barristers do and how their work differs from that of a solicitor.

■ What's the work like?

Barristers are specialist legal advisers and courtroom advocates: they are lawyers whom other lawyers consult on a specific issue, whether for advice or to make use of their advocacy skills. As suggested in Chapter 1, their work compares with that of consultants or surgeons in the medical profession, whereas the work of a solicitor compares to that of a GP.

Just as the usual route to a consultant is through a referral from a GP, so the usual route to a barrister is through a solicitor (although there are a few exceptions to this – see Chapter 1): the Bar is a referral profession, so members of the public cannot generally directly engage a barrister. Solicitors will have good working relationships with barristers and are likely to know or be able to find out the most suitable barrister to deal with a particular case.

Barristers work as individual practitioners: they cannot form partnerships with other lawyers and are responsible for their own caseload. They do, however, form groups known as **chambers** or **sets** in which a number of barristers have their offices in the same building and share the administrative expenses of clerks and facilities – but these are not firms. Every chamber has an experienced barrister at its head; there will be a number of other members of varying seniority – permanent members of a set of chambers are known as **tenants** and temporary members are known as **squatters**.

Barristers are independent and objective, and will advise a client on the strengths and weaknesses of the case. Unlike solicitors, they automatically have rights of audience (ie the right to appear and present a case) in any court in the land. When a barrister qualifies, it is said that they have been **called to the Bar**, which refers to the bar or rail which used to divide the area of the courtroom used by the judge from the area used by the general public: only barristers were allowed to approach the bar to plead (argue) their clients' cases. The term 'barrister' is derived from this usage of 'bar'.

There are two types of barristers: junior counsel and senior counsel. Senior counsel are those senior barristers who have been made **Queen's**

Counsel (QC) as a mark of outstanding ability. This is also known as 'taking silk', which refers to the silk gowns they traditionally wear – thus a senior barrister is often referred to as a **silk**. A QC is therefore a senior barrister who is normally instructed in serious or complex cases and would usually appear only in the higher courts. Most senior judges once practised as QCs.

Barristers tend to specialise in particular areas of law, for example civil law, family law, criminal law or immigration law. The work of a civil barrister may be divided into two types: contentious and non-contentious. Contentious work involves cases where litigation is contemplated or a real possibility. Non-contentious work involves advising on matters which have arisen not from a dispute between parties but often from a desire to avoid litigation in the future (for example the drafting of a will, the creation of a trust or advising on the terms of a contract).

■ Why engage a barrister?

A solicitor might want to engage a barrister for two main reasons. First, to gain an opinion on a matter of law from a person who is an expert or specialist in a particular field; second, to represent the client in court where the solicitor is not allowed to or would prefer a specialist advocate to take on the task. A well-argued case will impress a judge; good cross-examination will impress a jury. A barrister's specialist advocacy skills could make a difference to the outcome of a case.

When a solicitor asks for a barrister's view on a legal point this is known as seeking 'counsel's opinion'; where the barrister is asked to undertake litigation work in court this is known as 'instructing or briefing counsel' though the two expressions are often used loosely today.

If an opinion is sought the barrister will be sent the relevant paperwork and will research the area of law and consider the issues before expressing a view as to the merits of the case or what steps to take next. In many cases, barristers are able to give advice on a case simply by looking at the papers. In more complex cases, and certainly cases which go to court, it will usually be necessary to have a conference or consultation with the barrister, typically at the barrister's chambers. If counsel is instructed to act then the barrister will begin to prepare his or her arguments that will later be used in court. Thus most of a barrister's work will typically be centred on legal disputes. The barrister acts like the old medieval champion: stepping in to fight in the place of the client.

■ What makes a good barrister?

'You need to have utter confidence in what you are doing – or at least appear to,' says one newly qualified young barrister. 'You are absolutely vulnerable to the whims of the solicitor. You need to be flexible and robust.' A key skill for a barrister is to persuade, so strong communication skills are high on the list. You also need to be interested in people and business, and to be commercially aware (you will, after all, effectively be running your own small business). Below is a list of skills and qualities you might need:

- Good academic ability
- Flexibility and adaptability
- Written and verbal communication skills
- Numeracy
- Interpersonal skills
- Computer skills
- Independence
- Confidence
- Commercial awareness
- Meticulousness
- Energy and drive.

■ Who works where?

There are over 11,500 barristers in self-employed independent practice in England and Wales. Although some do a wide variety of legal work, many focus on particular aspects of litigation and the law, specialising in areas like construction, property, company law, crime, employment, personal injury, taxation, intellectual property or many other areas. Barristers also work for the Crown Prosecution Service (CPS), the Government Legal Service and Magistrates' Courts. Some barristers may hardly ever appear in court but spend their time writing opinions and giving advice on complex and difficult areas of law.

Most barristers practise from London but about 3000 are based in other cities and towns, including Birmingham, Bristol, Cardiff, Leeds, Manchester and Nottingham. All barristers who practise in England and Wales are members of one of the six **legal circuits** (geographical areas) into which the two countries are divided. The circuits are the areas around which the High Court judges travel to hear the most important cases.

Case Study

Paul is an experienced barrister who has been working from chambers in London since 1985. Most of his work is with insurers, giving them advice on whether or not they should meet a claim. He deals a lot with recovery work and employers' liability. 'It is very important to build up your reputation. This often starts with your clerk who will recommend you to do a piece of work from solicitors. After that you'll tend to

---

build up your reputation by word-of-mouth,' says Paul. 'Your task in court is to persuade the tribunal, so good communication skills are vitally important. You also need to communicate effectively with your own clients. A good grasp of the law and the enthusiasm to carry on learning is necessary.' A lot of stamina is required to be a barrister as the job is very hard work, often requiring you to work more than 10-hour days, sometimes six or seven days a week. 'Working from 6am until midnight is common, especially on a long case which can go on for weeks on end,' says Paul.

Because it is a tough profession Paul advises that you should give it serious thought. 'It's a very enjoyable profession. For people who like to be independent and work for themselves it's the ideal profession. But you need to be able to work on your own initiative and find a way of managing your work so that it does not entirely dominate your life'. He says you need a minimum 2:1 degree and advises you to do a mini-pupillage, preferably somewhere you plan to apply for pupillage.

For up-to-date information on law courses go to www.mpw. co.uk/getintolaw

03 How to qualify as a lawyer

Solicitor

It may come as a surprise to find out that there are a number of different routes by which you can qualify as a solicitor. Most of these are set out in the diagram below and then described in more detail in the text that follows.

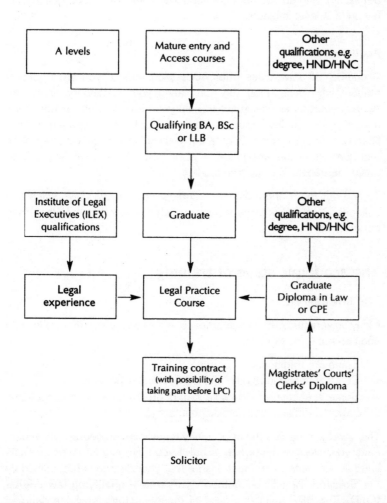

Before university

A levels

Nearly all A levels provide an acceptable grounding for a law degree. The traditional paper-based subjects such as History and English have an obvious appeal; languages may also prove to be very attractive to employers (particularly if you end up working for a firm with offices overseas) and sciences will develop logical thought and application, which are key skills for any lawyer.

The one A level which does seem to cause some controversy is law; some universities will accept it and others won't. If you want to study A level law and already have a university in mind, check with the admissions department that it would be accepted. If you are already studying A level law but have not yet applied for university then do your research before applying so you know which universities will accept your combination of A level subjects.

Access courses

A number of universities offer Access courses. If you are a mature student who missed out on completing your secondary education, Access courses are designed to help you move into higher education and on to degree-level studies. You may not have the academic qualifications of your fellow students but you will have acquired other skills and qualities in the workplace or at home and these will help you to make the transition to degree studies.

To find out more about Access courses, contact the universities and colleges in your local area to find out what they offer and when their courses run.

The academic stage of training

The law degree

Many universities offer law degrees, and these vary enormously in style and content – for example:

- Some are traditional in content
- Some enable you to gain real legal clinical experience
- Some enable you to obtain a joint degree (eg Law and Languages, Law and Politics, Law and Accountancy).

This variety gives you the opportunity to choose the degree which best suits your skills and interests – but if you have any intention of qualifying as a solicitor, you must ensure that your degree is recognised by the Solicitors Regulation Authority (SRA) as a **qualifying law degree (QLD)**. The SRA maintains a list of those institutions whose degrees are recognised as QLDs, so it's easy to check whether your preferred degree is on the list.

Having a QLD means that you have studied the subjects which the SRA considers to be the key foundation subjects for any lawyer. These are:

- Contract
- Tort
- Land (or property)
- Equity and Trusts
- Public law (constitutional and administrative)
- Criminal law
- European Union law.

The Law Society stipulates that your study of these subjects must account for about half of your total studies on a three-year law degree and, in total, at least two-thirds of your degree must be spent on law and law-related subjects.

Once you begin looking for a training contract (see below), you'll discover that many firms will expect you to have either a first or upper second class degree. You'll need to work hard right from the outset of your degree to maximise your chances of getting a training contract with the firm of your choice.

The exempting degree

The idea behind the exempting degree is to combine the academic and vocational (see below) stages of training. At the time of going to press, only two exempting law degrees are on offer, at Northumbria University and at Huddersfield University: the degrees are four years long and, on completion of your studies, you'll be deemed to have the equivalent of both a QLD (see above) and the Legal Practice Course (see below). The obvious attraction of the exempting degree can be the funding arrangements, although the introduction of top-up fees may have maximised this.

The Graduate Diploma in Law (GDL)

What do you do if your degree is in an area other than law and, on completion of your studies, you decide that your greatest ambition is to qualify as a lawyer? Luckily for you there is a course which enables you to convert your existing degree to something more relevant. This course is usually known as the Graduate Diploma in Law (GDL) – although you may also hear it referred to as the **Common Professional Examination (CPE)**. It is accepted by both the Bar Council and the SRA, so you can start the GDL without having decided whether you eventually intend to qualify as a solicitor or as a barrister, and then make your decision during the course of your studies.

The GDL is a one-year full-time course offered at around 40 institutions across England and Wales. Many of the same institutions also offer the GDL on a part-time basis over two years and, as with law degrees, the SRA maintains a list of all institutions which offer the GDL and in which modes.

The current cost of a full-time GDL ranges from around £4000 to £7500. You should check what the course fee includes – for example, some providers will include the cost of all books and materials within their fees whereas others will expect you to pay for these direct. Remember that you get what you pay for, so do not necessarily opt for the most inexpensive course. Look to see if the course provider has links with the professions.

Application for a full-time GDL course is made via the Central Applications Board (the CAB), which runs a system similar to UCAS. The opening date for applications is usually in November each year and the closing date is the following March; have a look on the CAB website, www.lawcabs.ac.uk, for more information. Application for a part-time GDL course is usually made direct to the institution(s) of your choice.

The non-graduate route

If you don't possess a degree, there are still a number of options available to you. If you work in legal employment, for example as a paralegal or as a legal secretary, you may decide to take the **Institute of Legal Executives' examinations**. The higher-level examinations are recognised by the SRA as being equivalent to a law degree and will therefore enable you to progress to the next stage of training, the Legal Practice Course (see below).

In exceptional circumstances, the length and quality of your work experience in any field, law or otherwise, may be recognised by the SRA as equivalent to a degree and could therefore permit you to take up a place on a GDL course. For more information on the non-graduate route to qualification contact the SRA, whose staff will be able to give you advice on your circumstances.

■ The vocational stage of training

The Legal Practice Course (LPC)

Following completion of the academic stage of training, prospective solicitors must complete a Legal Practice Course (LPC) at one of around 35 institutions across England and Wales. The LPC can be completed over one year full time or two years part time (in a variety of formats including evening, weekend or day-release study patterns). The current cost ranges from £5500 to £10,500 for the full-time course.

The LPC is made up of a combination of compulsory subjects and skills which you must cover regardless of where you do the LPC. You also take three elective subjects which you will be able to choose from the range offered by your chosen institution. The LPC is very different from the academic stage of training: you will spend a lot more time in small groups with other students and the skills content of the course means you will experience more 'learning by doing'.

As for the GDL, application for a full-time LPC course is via the Central Applications Board, www.lawcabs.ac.uk. The opening date for applications is usually in early October and the initial closing date is in early December for courses starting the following September. Applications for part-time courses are made direct to the institution(s) of your choice.

Case Study

Mark was always very clear about his career aspirations, but decided that in order to have the option of specialising in intellectual property he needed to complete a science degree as some of the work can involve patents and scientific know-how. He studied Chemistry at Imperial College and spent two years in London and two in Paris, where he did research and studied some French literature. Having planned with precision, Mark applied to do his CPE at the College of Law in London. 'I wanted to move back to London after Paris and wanted to be at the College, because it has a reputation for quality courses and is well recognised by leading firms. I had already started doing vacation placements at various firms and knew that although I enjoyed the research, long term I wanted to work in a profession more oriented around people.'

Mark found the CPE very fast paced and practical, which is excellent for a scientist who has always dealt with the practical applications of his experiments. 'CPE students do miss out a little on discussing the implications of law, but the practical aspects are great and really prepare you for life in a law firm.' Mark had always been part of a debating team, all through school and university, and when he arrived at the College he was keen to help give the debating team a boost. 'Debating introduces you to the skills of presenting your case in a logical way and in public. All solicitors need these skills as they have to talk to clients, think on their feet and justify their actions in an ordered and coherent way.'

The training contract

The final stage of your route to qualification as a solicitor is the training contract. This is (usually) two years of on-the-job training with a firm or other organisation which has been authorised by the SRA to take trainee solicitors. The SRA will require you to gain experience in at least three distinct areas of law during your training contract and to further develop your legal skills whilst doing so. You will also have to complete the Professional Skills Course (PSC), which includes further training and some assessment in legal skills. Your firm or employer is expected to support you through this process.

Depending on the sort of firm you want to go to for your training contract, you may need to apply up to two years in advance of your possible start date. This is certainly the case with the large City and national corporate and commercial firms, which will be recruiting as you are entering the final year of your law degree studies or starting your GDL. Other firms and organisations will recruit you as you are completing your LPC, with a view to an immediate start, so it is also common for students to start their LPC without knowing if they have a training contract to go to at the end of the course.

You can complete your training contract on a part-time basis and you can also combine your training contract with attendance on a part-time LPC. If you have considerable previous experience in a legal environment, then you may be eligible for a reduction in the length of your training contract, but this will depend on whether your employer supports your request. Any application has to be made to the SRA.

Funding your qualification

Qualifying as a solicitor has become an expensive business and it's not unusual for students to find themselves in around £25,000 of debt at the end of their LPC. So, what are your options?

Sponsorship

Many medium to large firms and other employers will sponsor you through the LPC and possibly the GDL if you have secured your training contract before commencing the course. The sponsorship will cover the cost of the GDL/LPC course fees and often a contribution towards your living expenses. You'll need to check whether the firms and employers that interest you would offer sponsorship of this kind.

The Solicitors Regulation Authority (SRA)

The SRA has a bursary scheme and a Diversity Access Scheme (DAS). The bursary scheme is aimed at students with a place on the GDL or LPC who can demonstrate a clear financial need as well as a commitment to a career as a solicitor. The DAS consists of several elements, one of which is a free places scheme with a number of LPC providers. For more details on both schemes, contact the SRA.

Access funds

These are available at universities and publicly funded colleges. They are discretionary awards aimed at assisting with your living costs if you are experiencing financial hardship. Details are available directly from your institution of study.

Career development loans

Once you get to the GDL or LPC stage of training, you may be eligible for a career development loan. For more information see www. lifelonglearning.co.uk.

Charities and grant-making trusts

Find out whether there are any such bodies in the area where you live and, if there are, check whether you meet their criteria for an award. Have a look on websites such as www.support4learning.org.uk for more information.

When you are looking for sources of funding, remember:

- Do your research
- Plan ahead
- Read the criteria for the grant/award you are applying for and make sure you can demonstrate that you meet them
- Don't be put off – you're training to be a solicitor so try to come up with a good case for yourself
- Be realistic.

Case Study

Karen is a trainee at Lewis Silkin, a medium-sized law firm based in the City of London and renowned for its specialist areas of expertise, in particular employment, advertising and social housing. Karen completed A levels in English Language, Law, Mathematics and General Studies. She obtained three A grades and a B grade. Karen went straight to Bristol University, where she read law. In her first year she read tort, criminal, public and property law. In her second she chose jurisprudence, contract, property, trusts and European law. In her third she elected to do medicine, law and ethics, intellectual property, revenue law, and gender and the law. She obtained a 2:1.

Karen seemed clear from the start that she wanted to be a solicitor. She comments: 'I wanted to be able to deal with clients from the beginning of a case and because of the possibilities for solicitor advocates nowadays it didn't seem to be closing any doors. I also dislike the stuffy traditions of the Bar.' Karen obtained a distinction on the LPC.

Karen also made sure that she gained work experience through summer work placements. 'After my second year at University I spent an intensive summer working for White and Case for two weeks, Barlow Lyde and Gilbert for two weeks, Olswang for three weeks and Mirror Group Newspapers (in-house legal department) for one week.'

Karen is in her first seat in the employment department at Lewis Silkin. She hopes to proceed to corporate as her next seat. A typical day in the employment department could involve her attending a tribunal, preparing documents for a tribunal hearing, interviewing a witness and drafting the witness statement, attending conference with counsel or assisting in negotiating a settlement or reviewing contractual documents, for example a contract of employment.

There are six trainees per year (that is, 12 at any one time) at Lewis Silkin.The favoured seats for a training contract are corporate, employment, litigation and intellectual property. In addition to the Professional Skills Course (PSC), Lewis Silkin conducts in-house training for its trainees.

There is a good induction programme at Lewis Silkin and a comprehensive system of support, so there is always someone to help you when you need it. However, because of the intense competition for training contracts Karen thinks you really need something to help you stand out. 'Being outgoing, having a sense of humour, and language and computer skills will give you the edge,' she says. 'My legal experience also helped enormously.' She advises, 'You must be very committed before going to Law School as costs are great unless you are sponsored. Be focused and persistent.'

■ Qualifying as a solicitor in Scotland

The legal system in Scotland differs from that of England and Wales and Northern Ireland. It is not possible to go into great detail in this book but here is a summary.

It is possible to study a Bachelor of Law degree (LLB) at ten Scottish universities. The LLB is offered as an Ordinary Degree over three years or an Honours Degree over four years. Admission requirements to all LLB degrees are high. After completion of the LLB Degree all prospective solicitors are required to take the Diploma in Legal Practice, which lasts seven months. The course has been designed to teach the practical knowledge and skills necessary for the working life of a solicitor. After successful completion of the Degree and Diploma, you need to serve a two-year post-Diploma training contract with a practising solicitor in Scotland. For further information contact the Law Society of Scotland. See 'Further information' at the end of this book for the address.

■ Qualifying as a solicitor in Northern Ireland

Again, it is not possible to go into detail, but here is a summary.

Law graduates who wish to practise in Northern Ireland should apply for the one-year Vocational Certificate course at the Institute of Professional Legal Studies, which is part of Queen's University, Belfast. Non-law graduates must complete the two-year Bachelor of Legal Science Studies at the same university before taking the Vocational Certificate course. For further information contact the Law Society of Northern Ireland. See 'Further information' at the end of this book for the address.

Barristers

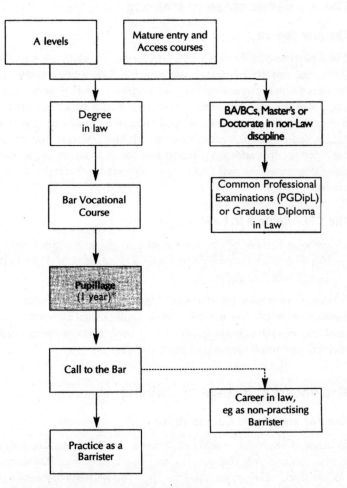

* 6 months non-practising; 6 months practising

■ Before university

A levels and equivalents

Nearly all A level subjects are acceptable. It is most important to achieve excellent grades, preferably grades A and B to stand a good chance of getting into a well-respected university and course.

Access courses

Many universities encourage mature students to apply for entry. Some of these mature students will have attended an Access course that has prepared them for higher education and further study. Previous relevant experience can sometimes put such applicants at an advantage.

■ The academic stage of training

The law degree

If you wish to qualify as a barrister you must usually be a graduate. Many, but not all, barristers will have studied a law degree (LLB). There are numerous varieties of law degrees, some concentrating on traditional law subjects, and others including a variety of options. It is important to make sure that you choose a Qualifying Law Degree (QLD). You can do this by checking with The General Council of the Bar (see for the address). Try to aim for at least an upper second class degree as you will find it more difficult to obtain pupillage with a lower second.

The CPE/Diploma in Law

A significant number of barristers hold a degree in a subject other than law. Again it is very important to obtain a good class of degree, ideally an upper second or above.

Graduates who have not obtained a law degree need to take an extra qualification in law. This is the Common Professional Examination (CPE) (also known as the Graduate Diploma in Law), which normally lasts one year full time or two years part time.

■ The vocational stage of training

The Bar Vocational Course (BVC)

To become a barrister entitled to practise, the Bar Council requires you to take the one-year (full time) or two years (part time) Bar Vocational Course (BVC). Before you start the BVC you will need to join one of the four Inns of Court – Lincoln's Inn, Inner Temple, Middle Temple or Gray's

Inn (all based in central London). These provide collegiate activities, support for barristers and student members, advocacy training and other continuing professional development opportunities. The Inns also provide the mechanism by which students become barristers, known as 'Call to the Bar', once they have completed the BVC and pupillage. The BVC aims to help you gain the skills of advocacy, conference skills, drafting, legal research, negotiation and opinion writing to prepare you for the practical stage of training on the job, the one year of pupillage. It is available at eight different teaching institutions throughout the country; see the list on page 33. Prior to 1997 the Inns of Court School of Law was the only provider.

Pupillage

Pupillage is the final stage to qualifying as a barrister and is hard work. The first six months of pupillage are non-practising and involve training with a senior barrister (your 'pupil master') at work for six months (unpaid). During the first six months you will be expected to undertake legal research, draft opinions, and read your pupil master's paperwork. Once you have completed the first six months, you will spend the second six months practising and be able to appear in court as an advocate. This is when you start to build your own reputation and have your own cases.

Those of you eager to become a barrister are in for a tough time. Competition for places is keen. In the 2007/08 academic year there will be around 700 places. On completion of the BVC, a high proportion of people will be unable to get 'pupillage' but may be able to work for a legal department in a major company. Full details about each institution can be found at www.lawzone.co.uk/barcouncil.

In 2001, the Bar Council introduced a new pupillage application system. All pupillage vacancies are now advertised on the OLPAS (Online Pupillage Application System) website – www.olpas.co.uk. *The Pupillage & Awards Handbook* acts as a companion to the OLPAS website. OLPAS allows you to submit online applications to up to 12 sets of chambers in each recruitment season. Before applying find out as much as possible about your preferred set of chambers. You can access the chambers' website or online Bar Directory, or attend a Pupillage Fair. For dates and venues of Fairs see www.doctorjob.com/barrister.

Case Study

Kim ran her own prosperous car spraying business for five years before deciding to embark on the long and uncertain route to the Bar. She successfully completed the BVC at the College of Law and is now on her first six-month pupillage. Why was Kim so determined to become a barrister? 'One of the options in my Institute of the

---

Motor Industry exams focused on law and I've been fascinated by it ever since. The experiences of a friend who is a barrister also inspired me – what also appealed was the variety of work you deal with, being self-employed and the challenges that the Bar presents.'

Kim gave up her business to undertake a law degree at Middlesex University as a mature student. She was keen to gain experience from different sets of chambers. 'I prepared early and spent a lot of time during the third year of university applying for mini-pupillages – I did 14 before starting at The College of Law. It gave me the ideal opportunity to learn about different chambers, what kind of work they do and how they function.' Kim chose to study the BVC at the College the first year the course was offered. 'The course was opening up to new providers and I wanted to be part of the innovative teaching methods that were being offered by the College. I also chose The College of Law because of its reputation in the legal community.' The BVC was a challenge. The sheer volume of work and the fact that she was constantly learning new skills made it hard, but also rewarding. 'Overall I really enjoyed the course. It was hard work, especially learning new skills such as drafting and opinion writing. Everything had a practical approach, which is different from most academic study. We also worked in small groups, which was an excellent way to practise these new skills.'

Funding

Money is an extra hurdle. You'll need a fair amount of it to see you through since the fees alone for the BVC are in the region of £9,000–£15,000. Those without a Qualifying Law Degree will have an extra year's training to pay for when studying for the Graduate Diploma in Law. The average cost of completing the vocational stage of training is estimated at over £20,000 if living expenses are taken into account. Only a limited number of awards, grants and scholarships are available for the vocational stage of Bar training. See the section on funding on pages 24–5). In addition, refer to the *Chambers Pupillage* and *Awards Handbook* and to the Bar Council Scholarship Trust – further details from the Bar Council.

Case Study

Claire is a barrister at Blackstone Chambers specialising in employment law. She was called to the Bar in 1998 and secured a tenancy with Blackstone that same year.

She chose A levels in French, Russian and Latin and obtained three A grades. Claire chose a BA in Law (European Option) at Queen's

College, Cambridge, spending her third year at the University of Poitiers, France. She got an upper second in her first year and a first in her final year. She later did a Master's in Law at Harvard, doing a mixture of antitrust and constitutional law/civil liberties.

Before going to Harvard Claire took a year off. 'After I left college I wasn't sure I wanted to practise law, so I spent a year working for Lord Lester of Herne Hill QC, doing political research and writing speeches on various topics such as human rights and discrimination. I then decided that the Bar probably was for me, so I went to Bar School.'

'In the summers after my second and third years at college I spent time at Simmons & Simmons in Paris, Baker & McKenzie in London, Freshfields in London, and Coudert Brothers in London, because at that stage I thought I wanted to use my languages and possibly work in an overseas office. I then decided to go to the Bar instead, and spent time before my fourth year at Monckton Chambers and Brick Court Chambers. During Bar School I did mini-pupillages at 2 Temple Gardens, Monckton Chambers, Brick Court Chambers, Essex Court Chambers and Blackstone Chambers.' Claire found her summer experience to be invaluable not only in giving her CV further credibility but also in helping her decide whether to be a solicitor or a barrister. 'I initially thought I wanted to use my languages, and being a solicitor was the only realistic option if I wanted to live abroad and still practise law. Having done a number of summer placements, however, I realised that I was perhaps not ideally suited to working in a corporate environment. I also wanted the chance, having formu-lated the arguments in a case, to be able to put them to a judge, and was concerned that if I did not at least try to become a barrister I might always have wondered what it would have been like. Finally, having decided, more or less on the eve of having to fill in the appli-cation forms for solicitors' firms, that I wanted to try the Bar instead, I spoke to my Dad who suggested that the Bar was too uncertain and a bad career for a woman – there was no better way of ensuring that his extremely stubborn daughter would choose the Bar.'

'When I was at Bar School there was only one option, namely the ICSL (Inns of Court School of Law). I spent a lot of my time that year doing part-time research jobs to cover the cost of the year over and above the scholarship which my Inn had generously given me, so I probably didn't give the ICSL a fair chance. In general, however, it was not a particularly interesting year.'

Claire's interest in human rights began at College, and her work experience with Lord Lester dealing with public law assisted her decision to focus on public law and employment law. 'I knew a little bit about Blackstone Chambers from my work with Lord Lester, and at the time I was applying for pupillage there were few chambers which were as good as Blackstone concentrating on commercial, employment and public law. Finally, when I came for a mini-pupillage I liked the atmosphere, particularly amongst the junior tenants. You need to enjoy spending time with your colleagues in every profession, but in view of the size of most chambers, and the slow rate of turnover, you have to be really sure that these are people you would enjoy going for a drink with.'

A typical day or week for Claire varies greatly depending on whether she is in court or in a tribunal – last week involved a conference with a QC about disclosure of the electoral roll and the ECHR; drafting an originating application to an employment tribunal in an unfair dismissal case; drafting grounds of resistance for a company on the other side of a similar case; settling a long-standing disability discrimination case for an applicant shortly before the hearing; preparing a judicial review for the Legal Services Commission; and preparing a possible injunction with a QC to enforce restrictive covenants against an ex-employee. It also involved various bits and pieces of advisory work, including advising on witness statements for a forthcoming seven-day disability discrimination hearing. Her hours are irregular and she frequently works in the evenings and at the weekend.

Qualifying as an advocate in Scotland

The intending advocate in Scotland needs to take an LLB degree followed by the postgraduate Diploma in Legal Practice plus one or two years' training in Scotland in a solicitor's office. It is advised that prospective advocates practise as solicitors for a period before going to the Bar. This is followed by further unpaid practical training called 'devilling' to an experienced advocate, in combination with sitting the Faculty of Advocates' written examinations. Contact the Faculty of Advocates for further information. See 'Further information' for the address.

Qualifying as a barrister in Northern Ireland

The Institute of Professional Legal Studies at the Queen's University of Belfast offers a one-year postgraduate course of vocational training for both trainee barristers and trainee solicitors. Anyone who intends to enter either branch of the legal profession in Northern Ireland must attend the Institute and successfully complete the course that leads to the award of the Certificate in Professional Legal Studies, which is a one-year course. Bar trainees spend a week work-shadowing a practising barrister immediately prior to commencing their course. A further period of in-practice training starts after graduation from the Institute and takes the form of a 12-month pupillage.

All applicants must hold a recognised law degree or hold a degree in any subject other than law and have successfully completed a course of legal study approved by the Council of Legal Education (Northern Ireland). For further information contact the Institute of Professional Legal Studies. See 'Further information' for the address.

■ Institutions offering the bar vocational course

BPP Law School
68–70 Red Lion Street, London WC1R 4NY
Tel: 020 7430 2304
Fax: 020 7404 1389
Website: www.bpp.com/law
Full-time and part-time courses available

Cardiff Law School
Centre for Professional Legal Studies, Cardiff Law School,
PO Box 294, Cardiff CF1 3UX
Tel: 029 2087 4964
Fax: 029 2087 4984

The College of Law
50 Chancery Lane, London WC2A 1SX
Admissions contact: Braboeuf Manor, St Catherines,
Portsmouth Road, Guildford, Surrey GU2 1HA
Tel: 020 7067 2400
Freephone: 0800 289 997
Website: www.college-of-law.co.uk
Full-time and part-time courses available

Inns of Court School of Law
4 Gray's Inn Place, London WC1R 5DX
Tel: 020 7404 5787
Fax: 020 7831 4188
Website: www.city.ac.uk/icsl
Full-time and part-time courses available

Manchester Metropolitan University
School of Law, All Saints West, Lower Ormond Street,
Manchester M15 6HB
Tel: 0161 247 3046
Fax: 0161 247 6309
Website: www.mmu.ac.uk/postgrad/bvc

University of Northumbria
School of Law, Sutherland Building, Northumberland
Road, Newcastle upon Tyne NE1 8ST
Tel: 0191 227 3939
Fax: 0191 227 4557
Website: www.northumbria.ac.uk

Nottingham Law School
Taylor Building, Chaucer Street, Nottingham NG1 5LP
Tel: 0115 848 2888
Fax: 0115 848 6878
Website: www.ntu.ac.uk/nls

University of the West of England, Bristol
Faculty of Law, Frenchay Campus, Coldharbour Lane, BS16 1QT
Tel: 0117 328 3769
Fax: 0117 344 2268
Website: www.uwe.ac.uk

04 Getting work experience

Getting work experience is crucial in terms of helping you secure a training contract or pupillage in today's extremely competitive climate. It is not enough to be purely a brilliant academic. The more relevant experience you have, the better the chance of succeeding.

■ What have you got to gain from work experience?

- It will give you a real insight into the profession and whether or not that is what you want to do. Some real experience will be particularly useful if you are trying to weigh up the pros and cons of qualifying as a barrister or solicitor.
- It helps you to make a better transition into your eventual move into the world of full-time work.
- It gives you the opportunity to build up those all-important contacts.
- It will help you to gain excellent references (hopefully!).

However, it is not that easy getting legal work experience. Most employers recognise this and do not stipulate that it is essential, although it is preferred. But if you can't get experience in a firm of solicitors or chambers, any work experience that demonstrates use of the skills they are interested in will be valuable. Skills such as communication, determination, business awareness and IT can all be developed in many other sectors of business and commerce.

You can also gain relevant experience and knowledge at university and/ or BVC by participating in debating, mooting, Inn advocacy weekends, mock trials and reading the legal pages in newspapers regularly.

■ Where to apply for work experience

- Placement in a firm of solicitors
- Mini-pupillage in chambers
- Paralegals and Outdoor Clerks
- Barrister's Clerk
- The Law Commission
- Law Centres
- Citizens Advice Bureaux
- Voluntary work in charitable organisations.

■ Marketing yourself

There is no one guaranteed way of succeeding in getting work experience, so try as many as you can think of and be creative in the process. Here are a few suggestions:

- Ask your teachers at school/college if they have any contacts in the legal profession.
- Use your Careers Service and speak to your careers officer.
- Talk to your family and friends and ask them if they can suggest anyone to contact.
- Make sure everyone you know is aware you are looking for work experience.
- Send your CV to firms of solicitors. *Chambers and Partners Directory* will give you names and addresses of solicitors' firms.
- Send your CV to chambers. *Chambers and Partners Directory* will give you names and addresses of chambers.
- Keep up to date with the profession by reading the 'quality press' on their relevant legal days and look at specialist journals such as *The Law Society Gazette* and *The Lawyer*, which should both be available from large public libraries.

Perhaps you could ask to go in for one or two weeks' work experience during the holidays or even ask for one day's work-shadowing to get an insight into what the working environment is like. Whichever route you take will almost certainly be on a voluntary basis unless you have specific skills to off, such as good office and keyboard skills, in which case you could try to get some paid work with a firm of solicitors during the summer or register with an employment agency.

■ How to apply

It's never too early to start to put together a CV. This is a summary of what you have done in your life to date, so if you have hardly any work experience then one page on good quality A4 paper will be sufficient. If you are a mature student with a lot of jobs behind you there is sometimes a case for going onto a second page. So what should go into your CV? Here are the main headings:

- **Name**
- **Address and telephone number**
- **Date of birth**
- **Nationality**
- **Education and qualifications**
  Start with your present course of study and work back to the beginning of secondary school. No primary schools please! List the qualifications with grades you already have and the ones you intend to sit.

- **Work experience**
  Start with the most recent. Don't worry if you've only had a Saturday job at the local shop or a paper round. Put it all down and try to draw out any relevant skills you have gained from it. Employers would rather see that you've done something.

- **Skills**
  List those such as computer skills, software packages used, languages, driving licence.

- **Interests and positions of responsibility**
  What do you like to do in your spare time? If you are or have been captain of a sports team, been a committee member or even Head Boy or Girl at school, put it all down.

- **Referees**
  Usually two: an academic referee such as a teacher or head of your school plus someone who knows you well personally, who is not a relative, such as someone you have worked for.

Always highlight your good points on a CV and don't leave gaps. Always account for your time. If something such as illness prevented you from reaching your potential in your exams, point this out in the covering letter (see below). Lawyers have excellent attention to detail so make sure your spelling and grammar are perfect!

The covering letter

Every CV or application form should always be accompanied by a covering letter. The letter is important because it is usually the first thing a potential employer reads. Here are some tips:

- The letter should be on the same A4 plain paper as your CV and should look like a professional document. No lined paper please! One side A4 only.
- Try to find out the name of the person you should send your letter and CV to. It makes a great difference to the reader if you can personalise your application. If you start the letter 'Dear Mr Brown', remember you should finish it 'Yours sincerely'.
- The first paragraph should tell the reader why you are contacting them.
- The second paragraph should give them some information to make them interested in you, eg highlighting your interest in law along with some specific IT skills.
- Say in the letter if you already know anything about the firm or have read anything in the press recently that was relevant.
- Employers accept typed letters, unless they specifically request one to be handwritten.

■ A sample CV

There is no standard CV but here is a sample:

PERSONAL DETAILS

Name	Simon Anthony TATE
Address	134 Hillhouse Avenue
	Portsmouth POI 2TQ
Telephone No	01245 879476
Date of Birth	10 June 1989
Nationality	British

EDUCATION & QUALIFICATIONS

2000–present	Linfield High School, Portsmouth
2005	A levels English, History, French
	Eight GCSEs English (A), Mathematics (B), History (A), Geography (C), Chemistry (B), Biology (B), French (A), Latin (A)

WORK EXPERIENCE

2002 & 2003	Delivering newspapers and magazines throughout my local area
2004 & 2005	(Saturdays)
	Sales assistant in busy dry cleaners in centre of Portsmouth
August 2005	Two weeks as a temporary receptionist in a small firm of accountants, responsible for answering telephone and general clerical work
SKILLS	Languages – good written and spoken French
	Computing – competent in MS Word and Excel

POSITIONS OF RESPONSIBILITY

	Captain of football team at school
INTERESTS	Football, swimming, reading, particularly Jane Austen, and travelling to other countries such as America and France
REFERENCES	Available on request

05 Choosing your university law course

In the late 1980s, demand for trainee solicitors briefly exceeded supply. Virtually anyone could pick up a training contract (then called 'articles') if they had the necessary qualifications. These days, however, competition is tough, and you'll need to show lots of ability and drive to impress your potential employers. The situation for budding barristers is similar.

But there is a positive side:

- Employers are generally impressed by a good calibre law graduate since law is known to be a challenging discipline requiring skills such as research, analysis, application, clarity, advocacy and effective written communication. These are very relevant in other jobs, so on the one hand you don't need a law degree to enter the profession, but on the other, law can be your springboard into a wide range of career possibilities.
- Some parts of the legal profession are growing, with law firms becoming more international and opening offices overseas (particularly in Eastern Europe) and expanding in areas such as Environmental Law and Intellectual Property Law.

The road to qualifying as a barrister or solicitor may not be easy, but the professional rewards can be great. If you are undeterred and still have your heart set on a law degree in some shape or form, then it's time to start thinking about your next steps.

What to consider

The basic criteria for choosing your degree course are:

1| The kind of law course you are after
2| Where you want to study
3| Your academic ability.

Going to university is an investment, so it is worth giving these points some careful thought. From the growing number of institutions offering law courses you will need to look at ways of narrowing down your options.

Once you have eliminated the bulk of the institutions and courses on offer, start to carry out your own research:

- Contact your chosen universities or colleges and ask for their prospectuses (official and alternative) and department brochures (if they exist) for more details. Remember that such publications are promotional and may be selective about the information they provide.

- Attend university open days if you can, and talk to former or current students. Try to imagine whether you would be happy living for three years in that environment and address issues such as: Is it a campus or in a city? Will it allow you to pursue your interests?
- Talk to any legal practitioners you know and ask for their views on the reputations of different universities and courses.
- Visit the websites of the universities you are considering.
- Find out what academic criteria they are looking for and be realistic about the grades you are expecting. Your teachers at school or college will be able to advise you on this.

Once you have done this you should be able to produce a shortlist of universities and from that you can choose the top five places to put down in your UCAS application.

■ Suggested timescale

Year 12

May/June: Do some serious thinking. Get ideas from friends, relatives, teachers, books etc. If possible visit some campuses.

June/July   Make a shortlist of your courses.

August: Lay your hands on copies of the official and alternative (student-written) prospectuses and departmental brochures for extra details. They can usually be found in libraries but it's better to get your own sent to you. Look at the university department website, find out when open days are being held and try to attend several over the next few months.

Year 13

September: Complete your application and send it off to UCAS – it will be accepted from 1 September onwards.

15 October: Deadline for applying for places at Oxford or Cambridge.

15 January: Deadline for submitting your applications to UCAS. They will consider late applications, but your chances are limited since some of the places will have already gone.

February–
April: Interviews may be held.

March: If you have been rejected by all of your choices, you can enter UCAS Extra, a scheme that allows you to apply to other universities. Contact UCAS (www.ucas.com) for details.

April: Decisions will begin to go directly to the candidates.

By 15 May: Or within two weeks of the final decision you receive, you must tell UCAS (assuming you've had some offers) which offer you have accepted firmly and which one is your back-up.

Spring: Fill in yet more forms – this time the grant forms which you can get from your school, college or LEA.

Summer: Sit your exams and wait for the results.

Results day   If you got the grades, well done! (UCAS will send
(August):   you confirmation of your place in September.) If you missed your grades, don't be too disappointed. Clearing starts straight away so don't waste any time – get hold of a list of unfilled places and contact the universities direct. You will be sent instructions on clearing automatically.

For more details about UCAS and filling in your applications see *How to Complete Your UCAS Application* (see 'Useful books' at the back of this book).

■ Different kinds of law courses available

a) Course content - Single or Joint Honours?

Qualifying Law Degrees are recognised by the Law Society and the Bar Council. This means that you can select the required courses that will exempt you from taking either the Common Professional Examination (CPE) or Graduate Diploma in Law (GDL) after you graduate. The seven foundations of legal knowledge are contract, tort (often both are referred to as obligations), criminal law, constitutional & administrative law (or public law), property law (or land law), equity & trusts, and law of the European Union.

Law can be taken on its own or mixed with a number of other subjects. It can be difficult to decide whether to study law by itself (a Single Honours degree), with another subject (Joint or Combined degree) or as part of a modular programme, alongside a multitude of topics.

If you are considering a Single Honours course, a good range of optional subjects might make it even more inviting. You don't want to be stuck with just a handful of choices from which to fill in your timetable after you've put down the core courses. And options may be law-related or from a completely different discipline. Some institutions can only offer a limited selection, while others provide a variety of law courses as well as the opportunities to take non-law courses.

Alternatively, if you want to specialise in one other area, then a Joint degree might be more appealing. Some Joint degrees do not require previous knowledge of the second subject. Others, especially those with a European language, often specify that candidates must have an A level or GCSE for background knowledge. With Joint degrees, be wary of courses that have seemingly identical titles, for example, Law with German, Law and German, and Law and German Law. In the first one, law is the major subject; in the second, you'll probably spend equal time on each and in the third the stress is on law rather than German language. Any of them may involve some time abroad.

b) Black Letter, contextual and vocational approaches

It is worth knowing that there are broadly three different approaches to teaching law – but you cannot base your selection on this criterion since few institutions adhere to one kind. Most places are likely to opt for a mixture (sometimes even within an individual unit, especially if it is taught by several different tutors). It can be useful, though, to find out (perhaps during an open day) which attitude is prevalent. The categories are:

(i) Black Letter Law
This focuses on the core subjects and doesn't look much beyond statutes and legal reports for its sources of law. It may sound dry, but it should provide a thorough grounding in the English legal system.

(ii) Contextual approach
Some courses examine law in context, that is to say, law, its role and its effectiveness are looked at in relation to society (past and present), politics and the economy. Such courses may include elements of critical legal theory. Students are expected to analyse the problems (for example, loopholes, contradictions, injustices and so on) within the law. This can make for some heated and controversial seminars.

(iii) Vocational approach
This stresses professional training and skills. It includes sandwich degrees with work placements, and other degrees with units dedicated to lawyers' skills like negotiating, interviewing, counselling, drafting, research, analysis, clear expression, and the ability to read through vast amounts of material, sift out the legally relevant points and present a logical argument. Ironically, you will be able to pick up most of these skills through other standard law units and extra-curricular activities like mooting (a mock court room trial), debating and Law Clinics, in which students get the opportunity to help out with a real-life case from start to finish.

c) Studying overseas and working placements

Studying overseas and/or completing a work placement could also be factors affecting your degree selection. Not all of these courses will send you off for a full year, though. Neither must you be a linguist, since you can study or work overseas in English in, for example, North America, the Netherlands or Malaysia. The availability of student exchanges has increased through programmes such as Erasmus, which encourage universities to provide international opportunities where practicable.

There are relatively few law degree courses which insist on work place-ments; however, some hands-on experience during holidays will prove invaluable and you should try to organise this yourself even if it is not a requirement of the course you choose (see the previous chapter).

■ Where you want to study

a) Which country and legal system?

If you're hoping to practise law, then ask yourself where you intend to work – England or Wales? Northern Ireland? Scotland? Since the legal systems differ over Britain, it seems pointless to study in Aberdeen if you want to practise in Aberystwyth (although, if you do need to move, then it is usually possible to transfer the legal skills and knowledge you already have and adapt them to the new place).

(i) England and Wales
See the chapter on how to quality as a lawyer.

(ii) Northern Ireland
Law in Northern Ireland is very similar to that in England and Wales, but if you study in Ireland and want to practise over the water, then you are obliged to sit an additional exam in Land Law. In 1977, the Institute of Professional Legal Studies was set up at Queen's University in Belfast by the Council of Legal Education. The Council runs a course that provides training for law graduates wishing to become legal practitioners. This vocational course leads to a Certif-icate in Professional Legal Studies. The core subjects you need to start the course are the same as in England plus Company Law (or Law of Business Organisations) and Law of Evidence. But if you haven't already done these then you have to take a preliminary course for a Certificate in Academic Legal Studies. After these certificates you need to find a two-year apprenticeship to get your Restricted Practising Certificate so you can work as an assistant solicitor for a few years before eventually becoming a fully qualified solicitor.

(iii) Scotland
Being a lawyer in Scotland (solicitor or advocate) initially involves passing a number of core subjects. The Faculty of Advocates and the

Law Society specify 11 common subjects plus two more each. After taking these within your degree there comes a one-year postgraduate practical course: a Diploma in Legal Practice. Beyond this, budding solicitors need a two-year traineeship to be fully qualified and advocates are required to do additional practical training and exams.

b) Various influencing factors

Once you've decided which country you'll be in, you can think about choosing specific institutions. But remember, university life isn't going to be solely about academic study. It is truly a growing experience – educationally, socially, culturally – and besides, three or four years can really drag if you're not happy outside the lecture theatre. Below is an assortment of factors which might have some bearing on where you'd like to study. See which ones you think are relevant to you and try to put them in order of importance.

Educational facilities

Is there a well-stocked and up-to-date law library nearby or will you have to fight other law students for the materials? Check for computer resources and internet connections, and availability of legal databases (such as Justis and Lexis). More vocational courses might also use mock courtrooms with video and audio equipment. The facilities available will depend on the budget of an institution, and plentiful resources tend to attract better tutors.

Quality of teaching

This is difficult to establish without the benefit of an open day but the University Funding Council, an independent body set up by the government, has done the groundwork for you and assessed the level of teaching across the UK already. Their findings are publicly available from the External Relations Department, Higher Education Funding Council, Northavon House, Coldharbour Lane, Bristol BS16 1QD (www.hefce. ac.uk). Teaching quality may suffer if seminar or tutorial groups are too large, so try to compare group sizes for the same courses at different institutions.

Type of institution

There are basically three types:

- **'Old' universities**
  Traditionally the more academic universities with higher admission requirements, the old universities are well established with good libraries and research facilities. They have a reputation for being resilient to change, but most are introducing modern elements into their degrees such as modular courses, an academic year split into two semesters, and programmes like Erasmus.

- **'New' universities**

  Pre-1992 these were polytechnics or institutes. They form a separate group because they still hold true to the original polytechnic doctrine of vocational courses and strong ties with industry, typically through placements and work experience. They are still looked down upon by some employers because of their generally lower academic entry requirements, but the new universities have a good name for flexible admissions and learning, modern approaches to their degrees and good pastoral care. Some law courses at these 'new' universities have been categorised as 'excellent' by the University Funding Council.

- **Colleges of higher education**

  Usually these are specialist institutions and therefore provide excellent facilities in their chosen fields despite their size. They are sometimes affiliated to universities (such as Holborn College).This form of franchising means the college buys the right to teach the degree, which the university will award, provided that the course meets the standards set by the university.

Attractiveness to employers

Few employers will openly admit to giving preference to graduates from particular universities. Most are looking for high-quality degrees as an indication of strong academic ability. But since students with higher A level grades have tended to go to the old universities, it is unsurprising that a large proportion of successful lawyers come from traditional university backgrounds.

Full-time versus part-time and distance learning

Although most students prefer to study full time and finish their degrees in the shortest time possible, some people, for a variety of reasons, find it more convenient to study part time or from home or via the internet. Only a limited number of institutions offer these options and they are listed in the guide in Chapter 3.

Guaranteed place on LPC

Many universities have an arrangement with the College of Law which assures a place on an LPC to every student with a 2:2 degree or better. This is a good safety net to have if you fail to get a 2:1, but if you think you will have a problem getting a good law degree before you even start, then ask yourself if you wouldn't be happier and more successful studying another subject.

Non-academic considerations

- **Finances**

  The cost of living isn't the same throughout the UK, so will you be able to reach deeper into your pockets for rent or other fundamentals and entertainment if you are living in a major city or in the South?

■ **Friends and family**

Do you want to get away from them or stay as close as possible? While there can be advantages, financial at least, to living at home, you may prefer the challenge of looking after yourself and the opportunity to be completely independent.

■ **Accommodation**

Do you want to live on campus or in halls of residence with other students, or in private housing that you may need to organise yourself and that could be a considerable distance from college? If your university is nearby, is there any point in moving away from home?

■ **Entertainment**

Are you going to be spending much time in, for example, the sports centre, the theatre or student bars? How about university societies– is there one that allows you to indulge your existing hobbies or the ones you've always dreamt of trying?

■ **Site and size**

This is not usually a problem since many universities overcome the issue of urban v. rural and small v. large by locating their campus on the edge of a major town (for example the University of Nottingham and the University of Kent), and centralising certain facilities and services to ensure safety, convenience and some sense of community even on the largest and most widespread campus.

■ Academic ability

For the majority of students, their A level scores will be the deciding criteria for selection. And it's important to be realistic about the grades you're heading for: don't be too pessimistic, but don't kid yourself about your 'as yet undiscovered' genius. Talk to your teachers for an accurate picture of your predicted results.

Not one institution requires law A level from potential students. Oddly, those applicants with a little legal knowledge might even find themselves at a disadvantage. Few courses specify subjects they want you to have studied (with the exception of most language Joint degrees), although traditional qualifications are welcomed everywhere. Conversely, some universities won't accept A levels like General Studies, or the less academic ones such as Art.

If your A level results effectively prevent you from taking a law degree, then it's time for a rethink. If you wanted to take a law degree with a view to entering the profession, then you could opt for the entry route with a non-law degree instead. Most employers stress that a large number of trainee solicitors and pupil barristers have a non-law degree. Even though the route might be longer and therefore more expensive (if sponsorship cannot be found), a graduate with, say, an upper second class Honours degree in philosophy is infinitely more likely to make a successful lawyer than someone who scraped a pass in their LLB. It is important to remember that since degree courses can change format frequently, you must check with universities directly to confirm their specific requirements.

Remember that if you intend to read a subject other than law, you will have to complete, following graduation in that discipline, a one-year postgraduate conversion course in law (CPE/Graduate Diploma in Law) before going on to a Legal Practice Course or Bar Vocational Course.

06 The UCAS application and the LNAT

■ Your personal statement

General advice on filling in your UCAS application is given in another guide in this series, *How to Complete Your UCAS Application* (see 'Useful books'). The advice in this chapter should help you write your personal statement. This is your opportunity to explain to the university admissions staff why you want to study law.

The personal section of the UCAS application is the only chance you get to recommend yourself as a serious candidate worthy of a place, or at least worthy of an interview. It is therefore vital that you think very carefully indeed about how to complete it so that it shows you in the best possible light. You must sell yourself to the department of law and make it hard for them not to take you.

For 2006 entry there were about 18,000 applicants for a law degree. Yet only about 15,000 of those applicants were successful in being offered a place. So you can understand how competitive applying for law is. Of those that were successful, nearly 2,500 applicants gained places through Clearing, and a high proportion of these would not have been placed at their first choice universities.

Obviously, there are as many ways of writing a personal statement as there are candidates. There are no rules as such, but there are recommendations that can be made. Universities are academic institutions and thus you must present yourself as a strong academic bet. The admissions tutor reading your form will want to know all the relevant information about you and will want some answers to the following questions:

- What is the strength of your commitment to academic study?
- Why do you wish to study law? Money, status, family traditions, the sound of your own voice and legal paraphernalia are not good reasons.
- What precisely is it about the law that interests you? Give details and examples, referring to recent cases, controversies and debates.
- What do you hope to get out of three years of legal academic study?
- What legal cases have you followed in detail?
- What related material have you recently read and why did you appreciate it?

- What recent judgments have you admired and why?
- What legal controversies have excited you?
- Which particular branch of the law interests you most and – again – why?
- Which lawyers, either living or dead, have inspired you and for what reason?

Work experience is very useful as it demonstrates a commitment to the subject outside the classroom, so remember to mention any experience, paid or voluntary. Explain concisely what your job entailed and what you got out of the whole experience. Even if you haven't been able to get work experience, if you have spoken to anyone in the legal profession about their job, then it is worth mentioning as it all builds up a picture of someone who is keen and has done some research. Wanting to be Ally McBeal or Rumpole is not a good enough reason to convince a hardened admissions tutor of your commitment to a law degree!

Future plans, if any, should also be included on your form. Be precise. Again this will demonstrate a breadth of interest in the subject. For example: '*I am particularly interested in pursuing a career at the Bar. My enthusiasm was initially sparked off by my active participation in the Debating Society at school, of which I am President. I also follow the major legal cases in the newspapers and have visited the Old Bailey on a number of occasions.*'

At least half of your personal statement should deal with material directly related to your chosen course, but the rest of the page should tell the admissions tutor all about what makes you who you are:

- What travel have you undertaken?
- What do you read?
- What sporting achievements do you have?
- What music do you like or play?

In all these areas give details.

> '*Last year I went to Paris and visited all the Impressionist galleries there. I relax by reading American short stories – Andre Dubus and Raymond Carver amongst others. My musical taste is largely focused on opera (I have seen 14 productions of* The Magic Flute*) and I would like to continue playing the cello in an orchestra at university. I would also enjoy the chance to play in a football team to keep myself fit.*'

This is much more impressive than saying:

> '*Last year I went to France. I like reading and listening to music and sometimes I play football at weekends.*'

General tips

If possible, use the UCAS web-based application system, 'Apply' (accessed through the UCAS website). From this year, it is available to private candidates as well as to those applying through schools and colleges. Print off a copy of your personal statement so that you can remind yourself of all the wonderful things you said, should you be called for interview!

If you are planning to do so, state your reasons for applying for deferred entry and outline what you intend to do during your gap year. For example, you might be planning to find some relevant work experience in a firm of solicitors, and then spend some time overseas to brush up your language skills.

■ The LNAT

The LNAT is the National Admissions Test for Law. It is an externally set test which is used by a number of universities to assist them in selecting suitable candidates either for interview or for conditional offers. It is used by the following universities:

- Birmingham
- Bristol
- Cambridge
- Durham
- East Anglia
- Glasgow
- King's College London
- Manchester Metropolitan
- Nottingham
- Oxford
- University College London

Details of the test can be found at www.lnat.ac.uk.

07 Succeeding at interview

The academic interview

Outside Oxford and Cambridge, formal interviews are rarely part of the admissions process. Even at highly respected institutions such as King's College London and University College London, interviews are not the norm for all candidates and are usually reserved for those from a non-traditional background and some mature candidates. They are expensive and time-consuming for both the university and the applicants. However, although academic interviews are rare, they do occur, so if you're invited to attend one, here are some points to bear in mind.

- Remember that if you shine in your interview and impress the admissions staff, they may drop their grades slightly and make you a lower offer.
- Interviews need not be as daunting as you fear. They are designed to help those asking the questions to find out as much about you as they can. It is important to have good eye-contact and confident body language and view it as a chance to put yourself across well rather than as an obstacle course designed to catch you out.
- Interviewers are more interested in what you know than in what you do not. If you are asked a question you don't know the answer to, say so. To waffle simply wastes time and lets you down. To lie, of course, is even worse – especially for aspiring lawyers!
- Remember that your future tutor might be amongst the people interviewing you. Enthusiasm and a strong commitment to your subject and, above all, a willingness to learn are extremely important attitudes to convey.
- An ability to think on your feet is vital ... another prerequisite for a good lawyer. Pre-learned answers never work. Putting forward an answer, using examples and factual knowledge to reinforce your points, will impress interviewers far more. It is also sensible to admit defeat if your argument is demolished.
- It is possible to steer the interview yourself to some extent. If you are asked something you know nothing about, confidently replacing that question with another related one yourself shows enthusiasm.
- Essential preparation includes revision of the personal statement section of your UCAS application, so don't include anything on your form if you're unprepared to speak about it at interview.

- Questions may well be asked on your extra-curricular activities. Most often, this is a tactic designed to put you at your ease and therefore your answers should be thorough and enthusiastic.
- At the end of the interview, you'll probably be asked if there is anything you would like to ask your interviewer. If there is nothing, then say that your interview has covered all that you had thought of. It is sensible, though, to have one or two questions of a serious kind – to do with the course, the tuition and so on – up your sleeve. It is not wise, obviously, to ask them anything that you could and should have found out from the prospectus.
- Above all, end on a positive note and remember to smile!

■ Preparation for a law interview

The advice below is based on the assumption that you will be taking a Single Honours law degree, but if you have chosen a Joint or Combined Honours course then obviously you will have to prepare yourself for questions on those subjects as well.

The interview is a chance for you to demonstrate knowledge of, commitment to and enthusiasm for the law. The only way to do this is to be extremely well informed. Interviewers will want to know your reasons for wishing to study law and, possibly above all, they will be looking to see whether you have a mind capable of developing logical arguments and the ability to articulate such arguments powerfully and coherently.

Much of the practice of law in this country rests on an adversarial system, so don't be surprised if you receive an adversarial interview. Remember to keep calm and think clearly!

Reasons for wishing to study law vary. A passion for courtroom drama, *The Bill* or *Kavanagh QC* is not enough. You need to think about the everyday practice of the law in this country and it is extremely useful to spend time talking with lawyers of all kinds and learning from them what is involved.

It is important to be aware of the many types of law that lawyers practise – criminal, contract, family, taxation ... and be clear about the differences between them. The essential differences between barristers and solicitors must also be clear in your mind.

Use of the media

As a serious A level candidate you should already be reading a 'quality' daily newspaper. The *Independent, The Times* and the *Guardian* all have law sections during the week. If you are really keen read *The Law Society Gazette* or *The Lawyer,* which are published weekly. Following detailed law reports in the press will give you further insight into the ways in which the law is practised.

Regular listening to the radio and watching television are vital. Much of the news has legal implications and these subjects are consistently discussed in the broadcast media. TV's *Question Time, Newsnight* and certain *Panorama*-style documentaries and radio's *The Today Programme, The World This Weekend* and *Today in Parliament* are all examples of potentially very useful programmes to help you build up a thorough knowledge of current events. Also regularly visit the legal websites mentioned in 'Further information'.

Knowledge of the structure of the legal and judicial systems is vital. You should know who the Lord Chief Justice is, who the Director of Public Prosecutions is and what he or she does. You should be aware of recent controversial legal decisions, who took them and what their consequences are or could be. Who is the Home Secretary and why is he or she important? What do you think should be happening in the prison system at the moment? What reforms would you like to see implemented in the running of the police force?

The interview

Interviewers will ask questions with a view to being in a position to form an opinion about the quality of your thought and your ability to argue a particular case. You may be presented with a real or supposed set of circumstances and then be asked to comment on the legal implications of them. Is euthanasia wrong? What is the purpose of prison?

Recent events are very likely to form a large part of the interview. Ethical issues, political issues, police issues, prison reform issues – all of these are possible as the basis for questions at interview. An ability to see the opposite point of view while maintaining your own will mark you out as strong law degree material.

Don't forget that interview skills are greatly improved by practice. Chat through the issues mentioned above with your friends and then arrange for a teacher, careers officer or family friend to give you a mock interview.

■ The interview for work experience

Most of the above-mentioned tips would equally apply if you are going for an interview for work experience to a firm of solicitors or a set of chambers. However, in addition you should:

- Research the firm/chamber thoroughly before interview. Look at their brochure and website.
- Plan in advance what you think your key selling points are to the employer and make sure you find an opportunity in the interview to get your points across.

- Prepare a few questions about the firm to ask your interviewer at the end. You can demonstrate your preparation here by asking them about something you have read about the firm/chambers recently, if appropriate.
- Dress smartly and appropriately. Lawyers tend to look quite formal.
- Remember a nice firm, confident handshake at the beginning and end of the interview.

■ Possible interview questions

Questions may be straightforward and specific, but they can range to the vague and border on the seemingly irrelevant. Be prepared for more than the blindingly obvious, 'Why do you want to study law?' question. But remember you wouldn't have been invited for interview unless you were a serious candidate for a place ... so be confident and let your talents shine through! Here are a few sample questions:

1| Have you spoken to any lawyers about their work? Have you visited any courts?
2| What makes a good judge/barrister/solicitor?
3| What area of law are you interested in?
4| What is the difference between the law of contract and the law of tort?
5| Have you read about any cases recently?
6| Should cannabis/euthanasia be legalised?
7| What are the pros and cons of fusing the two branches of the legal profession?
8| Should the police in this country be armed?
9| If you were in a position of power, would you change the current civil legal aid situation?
10| Should the police spend their time enforcing the laws concerned with begging?
11| What do you think of the recent law reforms?
12| What are your views on the handling of the Stephen Lawrence case?
13| Should Britain or any other country be intervening in situations like Afghanistan or Iraq?
14| What are your views on the right to silence?
15| How can you quantify compensation for victims of crime?
16| Should criminals be allowed to sell their stories as 'exclusives'?
17| Is it 'barbaric' to cane someone for vandalising cars?
18| How does the law affect your daily life?
19| What would happen if there were no law?
20| Is it really necessary for the law to be entrenched in archaic tradition, ritual and jargon?
21| How are law and morality related?

22| Do you believe that all people have equal access to justice?

23| What is justice?

24| Why do we send criminals to prison? What are the alternatives?

25| Should the media be more careful with the way in which they report real crime?

26| Is law the best way to handle situations like domestic violence/child abuse/rape?

27| Should British law encompass the laws of ethnic minorities since this society is so multi-cultural?

28| What causes crime rates to increase?

29| Should trial by jury be more or less common?

30| Do you think capital punishment should be reinstated?

31| Would the law in this country be any different if there were no Royal family?

32| You are driving along a busy road with the window down, when a swarm of bees flies into your car. You panic and lose control of the car, causing a huge pile-up. Are you legally responsible?

33| A blind person, travelling by train, gets out at his/her destination. Unfortunately the platform is shorter than the train, and the blind person falls on to the ground, sustaining several injuries. Who, if anyone, can compensate him/her?

08 The UK's legal systems

England

■ Current developments

The legal profession is constantly changing, so it is very important you keep up to date if you are thinking about a legal career. A good habit is to read the relevant press such as the legal pages of the major newspapers (eg *The Times* on a Tuesday). Also look at professional journals such as *The Law Society Gazette* and *The Lawyer*. The rest of this chapter outlines the legal system in England; here are a few points to bear in mind:

- Firms still place much emphasis on good A level grades in their selection criteria.
- There is some evidence that employers still look at the 'old' universities or what they perceive to be 'good' universities for their trainees. So in some cases students who had to study at regional universities because of financial constraints may be discriminated against.
- More and more students are completing their professional studies part time, mostly due to the lack of financial support.
- The number of students graduating from the LPC without training contracts is reducing. In 2006/2007 there will be 8919 students on the full-time LPC, an increase of over 1800 from 2000. The number of registered two-year training contracts has also increased.
- For the 2007/2008 BVC, about 3000 applicants applied for 1600 full-time and 130 part-time places available on the BVC.
- Growth of paralegals: more paralegals are being recruited to do routine work. This is often seen as a way in for LPC and BVC students.
- Technology has overhauled communications by the introduction of email, voicemail and video conferencing as well as the advantages of the internet.
- Solicitors' firms have become much more international.

■ The court structure

The court structure is divided into two systems: those courts with **civil jurisdiction** and those with **criminal jurisdiction**.

Most civil cases are heard, in the first instance, by the County Court, but in cases where large amounts are in dispute, they will initially be heard in the High Court. Appeal from both the County Courts and the High Court is to the Court of Appeal (Civil Division).

All minor criminal matters are dealt with by the Magistrates' Court. Serious cases are referred to the Crown Court. Here, the case will be decided upon by a lay jury, the essential element of the Common Law system. Cases can be appealed from the Magistrates' Court to the Crown Court and from there to the Court of Appeal (Criminal Division).

The highest court in the land, not only for England and Wales, but also for Scotland and Northern Ireland, is the House of Lords, which only considers appeals in points of law. Each case is normally heard by five Law Lords in committee. In 2005, 50% of appeals to the House of Lords were successful.

When a court is considering a European Community law point it may refer to the European Court of Justice in Luxembourg for interpretation.

The Judicial Committee of the Privy Council is the final Court of Appeal for the 24 Commonwealth territories and six independent Republics within the Commonwealth. In 2004, the Privy Council heard 68 appeals. By far the most contentious work relates to appeals against the death penalty.

■ Judges

In contrast with those of many other European countries, the judiciary in England and Wales is not a separate career. Judges are appointed from both branches of the legal profession. They serve in the House of Lords, the Court of Appeal, the High Court and Crown Court or as Circuit or District Judges.

The Circuit Judges sit either in the Crown Court (to try criminal cases) or in the County Courts (to try civil cases). Recorders also sit in the Crown Court along with District Judges, who also sit in the Magistrates' Court. In April 2007 there were:

- 12 Judges in the House of Lords
- 37 Lord Justices sitting in the Court of Appeal
- 108 High Court Judges
- 643 Circuit Judges
- 1201 Recorders
- 431 District Judges
- 28,253 Lay Magistrates.

Approximately 139 District Judges sat in the Magistrates' Court as at January 2005. District Judges are normally solicitors. Lay Magistrates are also known as Justices of the Peace.

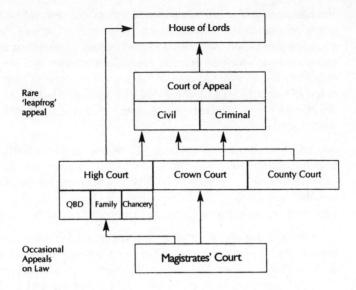

Outline of court structure

In fact, most cases are dealt with not by Judges but by lay people, who are appointed to various tribunals because of their special knowledge, experience and good standing. For instance, the majority of minor criminal cases are judged by Justices of the Peace in Magistrates' Courts. They are not legally qualified or paid but are respected members of the community who sit as magistrates part time.

All members of the judiciary are appointed by the Lord Chancellor, who is a member of the Government and also speaker of the House of Lords. The Lord Chancellor holds a function similar to that of a Minister of Justice, although some matters concerning the administration of justice are the responsibility of the Home Secretary.

Once appointed, Judges are completely independent of both the legislature and the executive, and so are free to administer justice without fear of political interference.

■ The future of trial by jury

When most people conjure up an image of a criminal trial, an integral element will almost certainly be the jury. The principle of trial by jury is rooted in the medieval origins of English law, and it remains a powerful part of the ideology of law. In theory, everyone retains the right to 'trial by one's peers', and jury trial is widely represented as a safeguard against oppressive government or the conviction-minded judge. But what is the reality?

The basic principle in criminal cases is that a defendant will be tried by jury in relation to any offence that is triable in the Crown Court. This court has jurisdiction over a wide range of offences, including the most serious crimes, such as murder, manslaughter, rape and arson, but also many lesser offences against the person or property. Even so, on average, less than 10% of all criminal trials are heard before the Crown Court, with the remainder being dealt with by Justices of the Peace in the Magistrates' Court.

Any citizen who is over 18 and under 65, who is not disqualified by virtue of some specific rule, may be required to do jury service. Juries are selected randomly on a local basis from the electoral register. If you are selected, you will be expected to attend your local Crown Court centre with other potential jurors. Each jury must consist of 12 persons.

It is the jury's decision whether or not a person is innocent or guilty on the evidence presented in court. The jury is advised as to the law by a professionally qualified Judge, but the decision on the facts is theirs alone. The jury's decision, or 'verdict', is given at the end of the trial, in open court. It must normally be a unanimous one, though in exceptional circumstances the Judge may accept a majority verdict. Where the result is a guilty verdict, then the sentence is determined by the Judge, not the jury.

One of the greatest causes of concern is the extent to which mis-conviction is the result of deliberate or negligent behaviour by participants in the criminal justice system.

Five years ago, the Labour government announced plans to end the right of trial by jury for some defendants. This was widely criticised, and the government suffered a series of defeats in the House of Lords. After some changes to the Bill, it was again defeated by the House of Lords in November 2003. Originally, the proposals were designed to save up to £100 million a year, but the changes to the Bill were watered down so that it would affect a more limited range of cases, including complex fraud and situations where 'professional criminals' might seek to intimidate juries. For updates, you should access the BBC website (www.bbc.co.uk), the *Guardian* newspaper's site (www.guardian.co.uk), or the Law Society's news section on its site (www.lawsoc.org.uk). Links to these and other sites can be found on www.mpw.co.uk/getintolaw.

■ Tribunals

A system of Tribunals operates alongside the court system. Each type of Tribunal specialises in certain types of cases. Almost all Tribunals have been created by statute. For example, Employment Tribunals handle disputes and all aspects of work-related incidents. This includes disputed deductions from wages, unfair dismissal, redundancy and discrimination. An Employment Tribunal is a more informal setting than a court. There are no Judges. Tribunals are headed by a Chairman who is appointed by the Lord Chancellor from a list of suitable applicants drawn up by the Independent Tribunal Service. In Employment Tribunals, for example, a Chairman will be assisted by two lay members. There is no standard form of procedure. Nonetheless, they operate in a similar way to court proceedings, with witnesses usually giving evidence on oath.

■ The Woolf Reforms

The Civil Justice System has always been seen as too expensive and too complex with long delays, which led to the radical reform of civil procedure by the Civil Procedure Rules 1998 following the recommendations of Lord Woolf in 'Access to Justice', 1996, better known as *The Woolf Report*. Criminal procedure was put under similar radical scrutiny in 2000 by Lord Justice Auld. His report was published in 2001.

Background to the Woolf Reforms

Lord Woolf identified several problems with the system of civil justice. His criticisms of the old system were that it was:

- Too expensive
- Too slow
- Too unequal – the rich litigant enjoyed an advantage over the under-resourced litigant
- Too uncertain – it was difficult to forecast the cost of civil litigation or how long it would take
- Too complicated – it was incomprehensible to many litigants
- Too fragmented in its organisation, as no one had overall responsibility for its administration
- Too adversarial, as cases were run by the parties and not by the court.

He contrasted these criticisms with the principles which the Civil Justice System should attain in order to ensure access to justice. The attributes of his idealised Civil Justice System are that it should be:

- Just in its result
- Fair in the way it treats litigants
- Efficient, in the sense that its procedures are appropriate and deliver justice at a suitable cost
- Efficient, in the sense that the system is reasonably quick
- Understandable to those who use it
- Responsive to those who use it
- As certain in its outcome as is possible in a particular case
- Effective, in the sense that the system is adequately funded and organised.

The Civil Procedure Rules

The above principles have generated the Civil Procedure Rules ('the CPR Rules'). These rules are based on the draft rules prepared by Lord Woolf which were published simultaneously with his final report. They represent a radical shift in the way that civil litigation has been conducted since they came into force on 26 April 1999, and consequently in the working practices of practitioners.

The underlying aim of the CPR Rules is to ensure that the Civil Justice System is accessible, fair and efficient. There is an overriding objective contained in the CPR Rules which enables the court to deal with a case justly by:

- Ensuring that parties are on an equal footing
- Saving expense
- Dealing with the case in a way which is proportionate to:

    (a) the amount of money involved
    (b) the importance of the case
    (c) the complexity of the issues
    (d) the financial position of the parties

- Ensuring that it is dealt with expeditiously and fairly
- Allotting to it an appropriate share of the court's resources.

The court is under a duty to apply the overriding objective in interpreting the rules and in exercising its powers. The CPR Rules also set out pre-action protocols in respect of personal injury litigation and clinical disputes. These are statements of best practice in negotiating, encouraging exchange of information, and putting the parties in a position to settle fairly.

The Woolf Reforms also changed some legal terminology. For example a Plaintiff is now called a Claimant. They also changed the way in which proceedings may be started. And they also imposed a duty on the court to manage cases in a particular way. For example, the duty now includes:

- Encouraging parties to cooperate
- Identifying issues at an early stage
- Deciding promptly which issues can be deposed of summarily
- Deciding the order of issues
- Encouraging Alternative Dispute Resolution (ADR)
- Helping parties settle
- Fixing a timetable
- Considering costs benefit
- Directing the trial process quickly and efficiently.

There are various sanctions for failing to comply with case management.

Claims are now allocated to one of three tracks: small claims, fast-track claims and multi-track claims.

- Small claims track – this is most cases under £5000
- Fast-track cases – these are claims between £5000 and £15,000, although cases of this amount involving a complex point of law can be allocated to the multi-track
- Multi-track cases – these are claims over £15,000 or complex cases for less than this amount.

Comment on the post-Woolf Civil System

- It is generally felt that the reforms are a qualified success.
- The adversarial approach has been replaced by a moral cooperation between parties, and the use of ADR has increased.
- The real issues of cases are being defined more quickly and this is leading to more cases ending in earlier settlements (rather than court-door settlements on the day of trial).
- The main problems are that:

  (a) the system is heavily front loaded, both in work to be done and in cost

  (b) new procedures, such as pre-action protocols, allocation questionnaires and case management conferences are more complex

  (c) the rules on time limits are not strictly enforced.

■ The Criminal Justice Act 2003

In November 2003, a new Criminal Justice Act received Royal Assent. The Act aims to strengthen the Criminal Justice System in a number of areas:

- The Act includes an exception to the double jeopardy rule for a defined list of very serious offences where new evidence emerges that strongly indicates that an acquitted person is in fact guilty of that offence and it is right in all the circumstances of the case for that person to be retried.*
- The Act allows witnesses to give evidence using TV links from remote locations if this would be more efficient or effective. In addition, witnesses' previous statements are more widely admissible at trial, including allowing witnesses to refer to their statement whilst giving evidence in court and greater use of video-recorded statements for crucial evidence in serious cases.

---

* *The first case where this law was applied took place on September 2006 and resulted in a successful prosecution.*

- The Act increases the maximum penalty for causing death by dangerous driving, causing death by careless driving while under the influence of drink or drugs, and aggravated vehicle taking where, as a result of the driving of the vehicle, an incident occurs and death results. The Act also amends the Firearms Act 1968 to provide a mandatory minimum custodial sentence of five years (three for juveniles) for unauthorised possession of firearms.
- The Act also includes changes to police powers, including extending stop and search powers for items intended to cause criminal damage, extending the circumstances in which the police may take a person's fingerprints or a DNA sample without consent, and introducing a power of arrest for the possession of cannabis, and it increases the maximum period of time that a terrorist suspect can be detained without charge from 7 days to a total of 14 days. (In November 2005 Parliament voted to increase this to 28 days as part of the anti-terror legislation introduced as a result of the bombings on 7 July.)

Constitutional reforms

In 2003 the Lord Chancellor's department was replaced by a new department called the Department for Constitutional Affairs. This is the latest development in attempts to modernise the English legal system. Government plans include replacing the House of Lords with a US-style Supreme Court, and abolishing the ancient post of Lord Chancellor.

Links to the latest news on all of the above can be found at www.mpw. co.uk/getintolaw.

The Scottish legal system

Scotland has its own legal system, with significant differences from those of the other constituent nations of the United Kingdom. The two fundamental differences are the role of the Scottish Parliament in formulating legislation, and the basis of Scottish jurisprudence in a mixed system of uncodified civil law and common law.

Since 1999, the Scottish Parliament has been responsible for legislating on a wide range of domestic matters relating to Scotland, but there are certain policy areas reserved for the UK Parliament at Westminster. Notably, these include constitutional matters, defence and national security policy, foreign policy, and fiscal and economic policy.

Scotland's legal system and court structure is separate and autonomous from that of England & Wales, and Northern Ireland. Historically, it has its basis in Roman Law, with some English Common Law influence since the Act of Union of 1707. Recent developments in Scottish law have seen the strong influence of English (and other jurisdictions') Common Law, as well as the influence and incorporation of European Union law. While some areas of law are similar to that of England, Scotland has its own system of criminal law and procedure, of civil procedure, and of certain areas of private law. The court system reflects these differences, with its own system of separate criminal and civil courts. By way of illustration, Scottish criminal courts do not have the House of Lords as the highest court of appeal, instead using the Scottish High Court of Judicature.

The legal profession in Scotland is divided between solicitors and advocates (the Scottish equivalent of a barrister). Qualifying as a lawyer in Scotland requires an LLB in Scots Law at one of 10 Scottish universities, followed by completion of the Diploma in Legal Practice.

The Northern Ireland legal system

Like Scotland, Northern Ireland (NI) has a legal system separate from that of England and Wales. Unlike Scotland, NI's legal system to a large extent mirrors that of England & Wales, with the following differences.

In terms of legislative law, the Northern Ireland Assembly (which gained legislative powers in 1999) has the power to make laws for NI, with the proviso that Westminster-created laws still apply to NI. The Assembly can, however, modify Westminster's provisions in so far as they relate to NI. Westminster also reserves a number of areas of policy-making for itself, including foreign relations, nationality and immigration, and fiscal and economic policy.

NI has its own court system (the Northern Ireland Court Service), which parallels that of England & Wales. It includes the High Court of Justice in Northern Ireland, the Court of Appeal, and the Crown Court. The highest court of appeal for both criminal and civil matters, as in England & Wales, is the House of Lords. Judicial law in NI is based on English common law and the doctrine of judicial precedent, and has developed on very similar lines to that of English common law. English precedent from the higher courts is not, however, binding, but is deemed to be persuasive. The higher Northern Irish courts also pay attention to important decisions made in the Republic of Ireland (ROI), the major Commonwealth nations, and even the USA.

As in England & Wales, the legal profession in NI is divided between solicitors and barristers. To become a lawyer in NI, an LLB from a UK or ROI university is required. After this, students complete a Certificate in Professional Legal Studies at Queen's University Belfast.

Legal terminology

Administrative Law: This is one of the core (or exemption) courses needed for a qualifying law degree. It usually teams up with constitutional law. It looks at the legal position of the government, public and local authorities and others who wield some kind of power over broadly defined policy, such as town planning and public health.

Black Letter Law: Means the fundamental areas of law, like law of contract, and equity and trusts. Doesn't include the more obscure or ephemeral law courses such as Feminist Perspectives in Law or Philosophy of Law. Tends only to examine law found in the law reports and statute books.

Civil Law: Unfortunately has several meanings. Can refer to Roman Law but it is more likely to mean either (a) private law, ie all law other than criminal, administrative, military and church law, or (b) the system of law which grew from Roman Law as opposed to the English system of Common Law.

Clinical Legal Education: This is the opportunity for you to get some hands-on experience with real-life cases without being able to go hideously wrong. Students, under supervision from qualified practitioners, give free legal advice to clients and usually see a case right through from beginning to end.

Common Law: This started about a thousand years ago in Britain. Up until then, each locality had its own customs and practices for dealing with problems and misdemeanours. So, Common Law was an attempt to iron out inconsistencies between different areas (basically so that the men at the top could ensure their incomes and maintain their power) by applying one set of rules to similar circumstances.

Common Professional Examination (CPE): This is the one-year course that non-law graduates must take to get on to the Legal Practice Course, on the road to becoming a solicitor. The fees alone are over £4000. You can avoid it by making sure you fit all the six core courses into your law degree.

Constitutional Law: The rules that control what the Crown, judiciary, Parliament and government do in relation to the country and all the individuals within it. But the constitution of the UK remains largely unwritten, unlike those of most other states, and comprises statutes, Common Law rules and constitutional conventions.

Contract Law (Law of Contract): There is an area of overlap between the laws of tort and contract. The same set of circumstances can even lead to tortious or contractual actions, so look up tort as well. Also, get used to this sort of far-fetched question: Adam has a TV which he promises to sell to Brian. Before he gets the telly though, Brian arranges to sell it to Chris for a tidy profit. But Adam changes his mind about the deal and sells it to David instead. When David receives the TV, it has been badly damaged in transit so he calls Adam to complain. Adam directs David to the small print at the bottom of the receipt that passes all responsibility onto the haulier, and so on ... Who owns the

TV and who should pay for the repairs? Yes, this is the kind of thing that tutors dream up to antagonise their students. It is an example of the law covering contracts, ie legally binding agreements (written, verbal or even implied) between two or more parties coming about as a result of offer and acceptance, although there are several other criteria that must be fulfilled too.

Core Subjects: Currently these are constitutional and administrative law; contract and tort; criminal law; equity and trusts; the law of the EC and property law. They make up a qualifying law degree that will exempt you from the CPE course after you graduate.

CPE: See Common Professional Examination.

CPS: See Crown Prosecution Service.

Criminal Law: One of the core subjects. Crime is so often sensation-alised that criminal law needs little introduction, but a lot of explanation, since the media continually obscure the legal points with hype. The law basically defines those acts that are seen to be public wrongs and are therefore punishable by the state. Most crimes are made up of two elements – the act itself (*actus reus*) and the thinking behind it (the *mens rea*), both of which must be proved 'beyond reasonable doubt' in court to establish guilt.

Crown Prosecution Service (CPS): Born in 1986, the CPS, headed by the Director of Public Prosecutions, is responsible for virtually all the criminal proceedings brought by the police in England and Wales, although the lawyers within the CPS don't always bring a case to court.

Delict (Law of Delict): Simply the Scottish name for tort.

DPP: Director of Public Prosecutions. See Crown Prosecution Service.

EC: European Community.

Equity: Half of the double act equity and trusts and one of the exemption courses. It is a (still developing) body of legal principles. It originated in the Middle Ages when, if you felt the Common Law was letting you down, you could petition the King's Chancellor for a fair appraisal of the situation. The Chancellor was keen to see justice done and wasn't too bothered about the rigidity of the law. Even now, equity prevails over the rules of law, but the system of equity is no longer as arbitrary as before. The main areas of equity cover trusts, property and remedies (eg injunctions). Look up the 'Anton Piller' order, that is a more recent example of equity at work.

Evidence: Remember that Tom Hanks film where the plot hinges on whether or not it's OK to use a crucial piece of evidence in court? Well, he lied in *The Bonfire of the Vanities*, and it was the law of evidence that he broke. This law covers the presentation of facts and proof in court. It is often associated with hearsay evidence that isn't always admissible, but also covers topics like confessions and the credibility of witnesses.

Exemption Subjects: See Core Subjects.

Jurisprudence: This is essentially the philosophy and theories of law. Jurisprudence units get right down to grass roots level and usually examine law from a number of angles, such as natural law, Marxism and the critical school.

Justis: This is a legal database giving you access to law-related information on computer. It is very similar to Lexis and Lawtel.

Land Law (Property Law): No points for guessing that this looks at who has rights (equitable and real) in different types of property and how these rights or responsibilities may be established or transferred. It covers subjects like mortgages, trusts, landlords and tenants, leases, easements and covenants.

Law School: Simply refers to the law departments within universities. Not to be confused with College of Law where students study their LPC.

Lawtel: See Justis.

Lexis: See Justis.

LPC: Legal Practice Course – the vocational one-year course after graduation (with a qualifying degree) and prior to the two-year training contract, designed for intending solicitors.

Moot: This is a mock courtroom trial. Some universities have specially made rooms for that really authentic feel, and others even go as far as to include video cameras to record your performance! But on the whole, moots are organised as extra-curricular/optional activities to improve your confidence and help develop your legal skills of presenting a clear, logical argument and questioning a witness.

Obligations (Law of Obligations): This is just another name for the laws of tort and contract.

Private Law: These are those bits of the law that are concerned with the relations between individuals that really have nothing to do with the state, but that doesn't stop the state intervening in certain circumstances of course. The areas are family law, property law and trusts, contract and tort.

Property Law: See Land Law.

Public Law: Sometimes this is the core course constitutional and administrative thinly disguised. Strictly speaking, public law also includes areas like tax law and criminal law, since they too are concerned with the relationship between the state and its individuals.

Statute: A general word for a law passed by Parliament.

Statute Book: The list of all statutes that are currently in force.

Substantive Law: Virtually all universities put most of the emphasis on substantive law at the undergraduate level. It is simply that huge part of the law that deals with duties and rights and everything else that does not fall into the category of practice and procedure.

Tort: Imagine it's a hot August day. You're gasping for a drink so you go into a café with your friend who buys you a bottle of beer. As you refill your glass you spot something a little suspicious and on closer inspection realise it's the decomposed remains of a snail! Do you:

(a) Drink the beer?
(b) Tell your friend to ask for a refund?
(c) Kick up a real furore and bring an action in tort against the manufacturer for negligence in production causing you to suffer shock and an upset stomach?

If your name was Mrs Donoghue and the year was 1928 then you'd go for option (c) and win the case, marking a milestone for the tort of negligence in English law! Tort is largely concerned with providing compensation for people who have been wronged and suffered personal injury or damage to their property through negligence, defamation, nuisance, intimidation etc.

Training Contract: The name given to the two years after an LPC when you train as a kind of apprentice solicitor. In some cases, you can reduce the time spent by completing work placements as part of an undergraduate degree, but even then the training contract will last a minimum of one and a half years.

Trusts: See Equity. Taking the simplistic approach, trusts arise when someone transfers property to you but you can't use it. This is because the property is held on your behalf by trustees until you're 18. The property is entrusted to these trustees until you are able to choose to dissolve the trust and look after – or spend – the property yourself.

09 Further information

◾ Useful addresses

Solicitors
Institute of Legal Executives
www.ilex.org.uk

Regulation Authority
www.sra.org.uk

The Law Society
www.lawsociety.org.uk

The Law Society of Northern Ireland
www.lawsoc-ni.org

The Law Society of Scotland
www.lawscot.org.uk

Barristers
The General Council of the Bar
www.barcouncil.org.uk

The Education & Training Officer
www.legaleducation.org.uk

The Faculty of Advocates
www.advocates.org.uk

Inns of Court
Gray's Inn
www.graysinn.org.uk

The Inner Temple
www.innertemple.org.uk

Lincoln's Inn
www.lincolnsinn.org.uk

The Middle Temple
www.middletemple.org.uk

General
Legal Action Group
www.lag.org.uk

Crown Prosecution Service
www.cps.gov.uk

Institute of Professional Legal Studies
www.qub.ac.uk/ipls

■ Useful books

There are a vast number of books written about the law and the legal profession and new ones are constantly being published. It is worth a trip to your school library, your local public library and your careers office to check what is available. Here are some we think might be useful to you.

The legal profession

Ivanhoe Career Guide to the Legal Profession, Cambridge Market Intelligence. (An overview of the legal profession)
Legal Profession, CSU. (The options from graduation to qualification)
GTI Law Journal, GTI. (Practical information about life as a solicitor or barrister, written by practitioners)
GET 2007: Law, Hobsons. (An overview of career options in law)
Law Uncovered, Trotman (What it's really like working as a lawyer, and tips on training, work experience and job applications)
Career Opportunities in the International Legal Field, The Law Society. (Opportunities for qualified lawyers and law graduates worldwide)
Solicitors' & Barristers' National Directory, The Law Society.
Chambers & Partners Directory of the Legal Profession, Chambers & Partners Publishing. (A comprehensive directory of firms of solicitors and barristers' chambers)
The Legal 500 by John Pritchard, Legalease. (A detailed account of the UK legal profession)
Solicitors' Regional Directory – Your Guide to Choosing a Solicitor, The Law Society. (A list of every firm in practice by region and town)
The Guide to Work Experience for Intending Lawyers, GTI. (Information on getting vacation placements and mini-pupillages)
The Bar Directory, FT Law & Tax. (Details of chambers and barristers)
Chambers Pupillages & Awards Handbook, GTI. (Details of chambers in England and Wales offering pupillages)
Prospects Legal, Central Services Unit.

General books on higher education

Degree Course Offers, Brian Heap, Trotman.
Directory of University and College Entry, Trotman.
Disabled Students' Guide to University, Trotman.
Entrance Guide to Higher Education in Scotland, Committee of Scottish Higher Education Principals.

Getting into Oxford and Cambridge, Trotman.
Choosing Your Degree Course and University, Brian Heap, Trotman.
How to Complete Your UCAS Application, Trotman.
Student Book, Klaus Boehm and Jenny Lees-Spalding (editors), Trotman.
Students' Money Matters, Trotman.
UCAS Handbook, UCAS.
University and College Entrance – the Official Guide, UCAS.

General books on law

There are a number of good introductory texts on English law and the processes of learning the law. Among the ones we would recommend are:

The English Legal System, Jacqueline Martin, Hodder & Stoughton.
An Introduction to Law, 4th edition, P Harris, Butterworths.
Learning Legal Rules, 3rd edition, J A Holland & J S Webb, Blackstone Press.
Learning Legal Skills, S Lee & M Fox, Blackstone Press.
The New Penguin Guide to the Law, John Pritchard, Penguin.

Miscarriages of justice and the legal system

Blind Justice, John Eddleston, ABC-CLIO.
The Law Machine, Marcel Berlins and Clare Dyer, Penguin.
More Rough Justice, P Hill & M Young, Penguin.
Presumed Guilty: British Legal System Exposed, M Mansfield, Heinemann.
Standing Accused, M McConville et al., Clarendon Press.
Report of the Royal Commission on Criminal Justice, Runciman Commission, HMSO, 1993.
Justice in Error, C Walker & K Starmer (eds), Blackstone Press.

Trial by jury

Jury Trial, J Baldwin & M McConville, Oxford University Press.
Justice in Error, C Walker & K Starmer (eds), Blackstone Press.
A Matter of Justice, M Zander, Oxford University Press.

Civil legal aid

Smith & Bailey on the Modern English Legal System, S H Bailey & M J Gunn, Sweet & Maxwell, 1991.
Achieving Civil Justice, R Smith (ed), Legal Action Group.
Tomorrow's Lawyers, P A Thomas (ed), Blackwell.

Professional journals

Commercial Lawyer: A monthly magazine
The Law Society Gazette: Available from the Law Society

The Lawyer: A weekly newspaper for solicitors and barristers, www.the-lawyer.co.uk
Legal Action: Bulletin of the Legal Action Group
Legal Business: Available from Legalease
The Economist

National press

The Times (Tuesday)
The Independent (Wednesday)

■ Useful legal websites

Note that addresses may change.

Legal publishers

Butterworths: www.butterworths.co.uk
GTI: www.gti.co.uk
Legalease: www.legalease.co.uk

General

www.infolaw.co.uk
www.online-law.co.uk
www.prospects.ac.uk
www.bbc.co.uk

Education/training

www.bppls.com
www.bvconline.co.uk
www.lawcabs.ac.uk
www.lawcol.org.uk
www.olpas.co.uk
www.pupillages.com

Careers

www.chambersandpartners.com
www.lawcareers.net
www.lcan.org.uk
www.simplylawjobs.com